Good Night

St. Martin's Griffin
New York

Good Nights

The

Happy Parents' Guide

to the Family Bed

(and a Peaceful Night's Sleep!)

JAY GORDON, M.D., and MARIA
GOODAVAGE

Excerpt from *I Know Why the Caged Bird Sings* by Maya Angelou. Copyright © 1969 by Maya Angelou. Used by permission of Random House, Inc.

Excerpt from *Dr. Ruth's Pregnancy Guide for Couples* by Ruth K. Westheimer and Amos Grunebaüm, M.D. Copyright © 1999. Used by permission of Taylor & Francis/Routledge, Inc.

Excerpt from "Co-Sleeping: Can We Ever Put the Issue to Rest?" by Jane E. Anderson, M.D., in *Contemporary Pediatrics*, June 1, 2000. Copyright © 2000. Used by permission of *Contemporary Pediatrics*.

www.stmartins.com

Book design by Claire Vaccaro
Illustrations by Phil Frank

Library of Congress Cataloging-in-Publication Data

Gordon, Jay.
    Good nights : the happy parents' guide to the family bed (and a peaceful night's sleep!) Jay Gordon and Maria Goodavage.--1st ed.
        p. cm.
    Includes bibliographical references (p. 207) and index (p. 215).
    ISBN 978-0-312-27518-1
        1. Children—Sleep. 2. Infants—Care. I. Goodavage, Maria. II. Title.

RJ506.S55 G67 2002
649'.122—dc21   2001059887

First Edition: July 2002

D 20 19 18 17 16 15 14

To my wife, Meyera, and my daughter, Simone.

I love you.

J.N.G.

To my husband, Craig, and my daughter, Laura,

who laughs joyously in her sleep.

M.G.

Contents

Contents

Acknowledgments

The birth of a book always involves so many more people than just the authors. Because this book contains so much new information, a huge amount of work went into its research and its writing. It was a labor of love with a long gestation period. We couldn't have delivered it without the help of dozens—actually hundreds—of people. Here are some to whom we're deeply grateful.

We are especially indebted to anthropologist James McKenna, Ph.D., who heads the Mother-Baby Behavioral Sleep Laboratory at the University of Notre Dame. His revered scientific work on co-sleeping has spawned a whole new field of research. Even though he was working on a book of his own at the time, he was incomparably generous with providing us with priceless research and papers, some of which hadn't even been published yet. "The more books on the subject, the better," he'd say. "People need to know about this." We will never forget his kindness and generosity.

Acknowledgments

We're also very thankful to David Servan-Schreiber, M.D., Ph.D., a neuroscientist and psychiatrist who really knows how people—and books—tick. His opinions on the manuscript, and his contributions, were invaluable.

Special thanks to Pam Oselka, of the La Leche League International Alumnae Association, and to La Leche League International itself, for helping us reach hundreds of family bed "alum."

Also much gratitude to the dynamic Janet Jendron, mother of four former family bedders, who helped us get in touch with the world.

Along these lines, we want to thank Barbara Nicholson and Lysa Parker, cofounders of Attachment Parenting International. They put out the call to parents, and parents responded. They also gave us some really good ideas.

We thank and hold in great esteem William Sears, M.D., and Tine Thevenin. Their earlier works on the family bed have helped countless parents get comfortable with the idea of co-sleeping. They bravely broke the ground before co-sleeping began its journey out of the closet.

We're very grateful to our wonderful agent, Carol Mann, who pitched well and saw us through some unique moments.

We also wish to thank Steve Cohen, M.D., a family practitioner, for sharing his extensive experiences, both personal and professional.

Hats off to Richard Leiby, of the *Washington Post*, who helped us come up with a winning title, despite his feelings about the family bed. (We're just "cribbing" you, Rich.)

We're deeply appreciative of brilliant science writer Keay Davidson's encouragement about the basic premise of the book

Acknowledgments

when it was in its embryonic stages, and of his advice about ways to handle the book's scientific aspects.

Finally, we are profoundly indebted to the hundreds of family bedders who participated in our questionnaire and who talked with us about their experiences for this book. They are the true experts.

Some notes from Dr. Jay:

Thanks to Maria Goodavage. We make a good book team.

A huge thanks to my incredible office support team who make my job easier and talked to parents about sleep every day: Ileana Hernandez, Christy Whiteside, Beverly Kitz, Marci Tarle, Jennifer Davidson, Holly Factor, Harriet Cutler, and Lisa Boehle.

And a very special thanks to my associate and office mate Linda Nussbaum, M.D., F.A.A.P., for being an excellent doctor and taking wonderful care of our shared patients for years and years.

I am grateful to the terrific families in my practice, who have taught me more over the years about the family bed and great parenting than I learned anywhere else.

And, again and again, thank you, Meyera, for your love and help, and, Simone, for being the best daughter in the world.

And a few words from Maria:

Big thanks to Dr. Jay, a terrific coauthor.

Grazie molto to my own wonderful mother, Evelyn, who put in countless Grammy hours with Laura while I was working on the book. Also, for her amazing ability to ferret out information about famous folk. Even through her fight with cancer, she was always there for me and for this project. She is truly an astounding woman.

Special thanks to Therese Hong, a great mom and an old friend. Although relatively new to the family bed, she provided me with some extraordinary insights.

I'm also very grateful to Rosemary Nocera, who pinch-hit when she was really needed. And to Melanie Fife, who should write, and Sally Deneen, who does.

For her inspiration, I wish to thank Franca, my younger Italian aunt, who showed me long ago that children who slept in the same room as their parents can grow up to be amazing adults.

And mostly, I couldn't have done it without the love and support of my husband, Craig Hanson, who gave many squishy (and often fishy, after a day of pursuing salmon) family hugs with the other half of my household support team—my sweet and life-loving daughter, Laura. I couldn't ask for a better family.

Introduction

Most babies don't come into the world terribly aware of the popular phrase "Sleeps like a baby."

But most parents would really, really like their infant to sleep like the mythical baby in this expression. After all, staying sane and happy in a child's formative years is important, and getting some sleep can do much toward those goals.

Sleep is such a huge concern of parents that if I didn't have to talk about it during my patients' checkups at two months of age, four months, six months, and all the way through to the five-year-old visit, I think I could finish my office day by noon!

Unfortunately, many tired and frustrated parents in our culture rush out and buy one or two of many popular sleep-training books, which generally instruct parents how to let babies cry alone in their cribs until they "learn" how to sleep.

But there's another way for everyone to get more sleep. It's kinder, gentler, easy on your mind and body, and it usually feels so right to baby and parents. It's been around since before humans were humans and is still practiced in most parts of this planet.

It goes by many names: Co-sleeping, bed sharing, sleep sharing, the family bed.

Simply put, the baby shares your bed. It makes nighttime much easier. In fact, it can make nighttime positively blissful. (How many parents of cribbed infants can say this?)

But even more than this, new scientific discoveries are revealing that babies were meant to be beside parents at night. A few surprising benefits of co-sleeping:

- The family bed offers many protections that can actually help save a baby's life. (I firmly believe a safely set up family bed is safer than solitary infant sleep.)
- Family bed babies cry less than babies who sleep alone—a boon to both babies and parents.
- Family bed children end up more independent and better adjusted later in life than those who slept without parental contact.

And this will knock your socks off:

- Most family bed parents have very satisfying sex lives. This finding demolishes the nagging myth that the family bed spells death to sex!

My patients taught me about the family bed. They showed me that it was a safe, flexible, and healthy alternative to the rigid sleep habits I had been told to dictate to the parents in my practice.

Introduction

In medical training we often learn to give advice based on theoretical "science" rather than by looking at the practical aspects of taking care of families and children. Watching moms and dads and babies work out their own sleeping arrangements and patterns helped me understand the many different answers to questions about sleep.

In my practice, and in TV and radio appearances, I stress to parents just how safe a safely set up family bed is. The new scientific findings underscore what I've been witnessing for decades. I have never had a single crib death in all my years of practice, and I can assure you that it's not because of any spectacular skills I have at preventing SIDS (Sudden Infant Death Syndrome). It's because the parents in my practice almost all sleep with or very near their babies.

I never recommend separate rooms for newborns and parents. Never.

I have wanted to write this book for many years but I needed Maria Goodavage. Her journalistic background and experience with her first child moved her to do extensive research on the topic; then she found me to be her medical support and coauthor.

If your baby could talk, she'd beg you to read this book. If she could read, she'd do it for you.

Enjoy. And savor the extra time you'll get to cuddle with your little one. They really do grow up so fast.

1.

Baby Knows Best

And You Should Listen

Science is finally beginning to discover what babies have known all along: Babies are designed to sleep with their parents. And parents are designed to sleep with their babies.

At the Mother-Baby Behavioral Sleep Laboratory at the University of Notre Dame, anthropologist James McKenna, Ph.D., watches an intimate dance unfold. It's a dance in which there's no leader, no follower, and yet almost seamless choreography.

A mother and father sleep with their baby between them in a large bed in the laboratory's comfortable bedroom. It's similar to the way they sleep at home, only with infrared video cameras monitoring their sleep stages, zooming in on every roll of an eyeball, every twitch of muscle, all night long.

All is quiet and still, except for the rapidly moving, closed eyes of the baby, mother, and father. They're all dreaming at the same time. Moments later they enter a stage of light sleep together: The mother stirs, awakens for just a moment, and drifts back to sleep, moving her head a little to the left, her arm to the right. The baby stirs, moves her head to the left, her arm to the right. Then the father follows with the same pattern. McKenna, director of the lab, smiles broadly and nods his head.

"It's incredible watching these sequences unfold," says McKenna, acclaimed as the father of this type of sleep research, and the world's foremost authority on the biological basis of co-sleeping. "The synchronization that happens when parents sleep beside their baby is remarkable."

Similar experiments in England find the same dance with family bedders. But place the baby in another room, and it's like putting a wall between a pair of ballroom dancers. Everyone reverts to their own rhythms, their sleep cycles coinciding only by chance.

The beauty of this natural nocturnal waltz rests not only in its well-matched moves, but also in its value for the baby: It turns out to be a great life enhancer. Some researchers say it even has the potential to be a lifesaver.

Born Before Their Time

Human infants are extremely immature at birth. Even when born at full term, our babies are frightfully ill-equipped to survive without almost constant care. Most mammals are born with 60 to 90 percent of their brain volume and can be independent of their parents within a year.

But not human infants. Born with a mere 25 percent of their future brain volume, human babies are the most vulnerable, and most slow-developing, of all mammals.[1,2]

The human setup doesn't sound very sensible, evolution-wise, but nature has its reasons. Back about four million years ago, our ancestors started coming down from the trees and finding that walking on two legs (bipedalism) was of enormous help for a variety of reasons, including foraging, spotting predators, and later, for making and using simple tools.

This was a superb step in the right direction, but it came with a hitch: Bipedalism reduced the size of the birth canal. It wasn't a big deal until about two million years later when we experienced a rapid increase in our brain size (and the size of the head that held it). This made for a tough fit when it came to giving birth.[3] Eventually push came to shove, and something had to give. Evolution's compromise: Babies born with brains that were a fraction of the size they would become, saving most neurological development for later.[4]

As any woman who's had a baby in the last few million years can attest to, childbirth is still a bit of a tight squeeze—even with the adaptation of giving birth to babies whose brains are only 25 percent of their final size. Such neurological immaturity makes human babies extraordinarily dependent on their parents and begs for close parental contact night and day.

In this sense our nonambulatory, nearly helpless babies are born before their time. In effect they need to finish their gestation outside the womb.

Food, Shelter, Clothing . . . and Touch

The consequences of this immaturity extend far beyond a baby's need to get adequate nutrition, heat, and diaper changes. In the last several years, researchers from academic institutions around the world have demonstrated another essential ingredient to survival: caring human touch.

When infants in neonatal wards were placed in the completely controlled environment of an incubator, with a minimum of tactile stimulation, their growth rates were precipitously slow. Yet when caretakers gave these babies a few gentle massages a day, the babies rapidly caught up with their expected growth curves—their little bodies "nourished" by the tender touch of another human.[5]

A new wealth of scientific research is revealing just how essential a parent's physical closeness is to a baby. Being near a parent on a regular basis helps babies regulate many vital functions their fledgling nervous systems have yet to perfect, including heart rate and rhythm, hormone levels, blood pressure, and body temperature.[6,7,8] Exactly how some of this information is passed from parent to infant isn't yet clear. In most cases we can witness only the results of this intimate regulation, not the mechanisms behind it. But the results are nothing short of wondrous.

For instance, when a mother holds her baby in skin-to-skin contact, her body temperature fluctuates to keep the baby's temperature normal. If the baby is too cold, the mother's temperature increases. When the baby's temperature is normal, the mother's goes back to normal.[9] It's as if the mother is a ther-

mostat, effortlessly keeping her baby in the optimal temperature range. This remarkable synchronization continues as long
as the two are in contact.

The implications of such findings are profound, especially
for more fragile babies. When premature babies rest skin-to-
skin on a parent's chest for short periods throughout the day,
their heart rates and temperatures stabilize more quickly, they
sleep more deeply, cry less, breathe better, grow faster, and end
up going home sooner than babies who don't receive this
"touching" prescription.[10]

A mother's touch can even act as a strong analgesic for
newborns. Researchers at the Boston Medical Center found
that infants who lie skin-to-skin on their mothers' bellies
showed much less pain (crying and grimacing) during routine
"heel stick" blood draws than babies left swaddled alone in
cribs. Heart rates among the touched babies were also substan-
tially reduced, indicating less distress.[11] Since touch can be a
powerful pain reliever, babies who have more regular skin-to-
skin contact with a parent may have a higher overall comfort
level than their less-touched counterparts.

A NOTE FROM DR. JAY: *In my practice, I give all vac-
cines when the babies are in mom's or dad's arms. The
child feels so much better, and we don't have to deal
with as much fear.*

Touch actually rivals mother's milk as a baby's body
builder. In animal experiments, it took less than an hour of separation from the mother for the infant's level of growth hormone to start to decrease.[12]

Good Nights

In the early 1900s, many unfortunate infants perished when raised in institutional environments where all their "standard" needs were met but where they were deprived of touch. What had been thought to be the most beneficial conditions to an infant, such as sterile wards of an orphanage where the baby was rarely handled, proved fatal.[13]

With a need for contact so deeply ingrained in a baby's makeup, it's no wonder that newborns find it extremely stressful to be separated from their parents at night.

Some researchers have even suggested that the immaturity of human infants may be a factor in some cases of Sudden Infant Death Syndrome (SIDS). One theory behind SIDS is that some infants fail to rouse themselves from deep sleep during a drop in body temperature or a pause in breathing.[14]

But when babies share a bed with parents, they're partners in the nocturnal dance documented by McKenna. Stimulated by the parents' movements and sounds, babies tend to spend less time in deep sleep, more time in light sleep.[15] Although co-sleeping is not a magic pill against SIDS, it may offer some vulnerable babies protection by causing them to avoid long stretches of deep sleep.[16] In addition, family bed babies tend to sleep on their sides and backs, possibly because of ease of breast-feeding. This minimizes the face-down sleeping position, which is a known risk factor for SIDS.[17]

Philip, a father of three, is among several parents we've heard from who think the family bed may have been a lifesaver. His youngest child experienced many frightening periods of apnea (breathing cessation) throughout the night. "I'll never know if he would have resumed breathing on his own after all of those periods of apnea if we hadn't been beside him in the bed giving him a little nudge," he says. (See "Bedders Safe, Not Sorry," page 54, for a dramatic account of another infant whose life may have been saved by co-sleeping.)

It's intriguing that the rate of SIDS is highest in industrial societies where infants sleep separately from their parents. In societies where babies routinely sleep with their parents, the rate of SIDS is considerably lower.[18] It would be convenient to argue that the increased SIDS cases in modern societies stem from pollution, parents who smoke, or any of the environmental drawbacks of living in a "developed" culture. But Japan is the fly in that theory's ointment. Japan, where babies routinely sleep with their parents, boasts low SIDS figures more typical of nonindustrialized countries.*

In fact, when people from co-sleeping countries move to the United States, their SIDS rates start out low; but the longer they live in the United States, the higher the rate of SIDS.[19] The "Americanization" of their sleep habits, with solitary infant sleep replacing co-sleeping, could be a contributing factor to this tragic increase.

We have only to look to other primates—our closest cousins—to get an idea of what kind of sleeping arrangements have carved their biological impression into our family tree: Without exception, all other higher primates maintain direct, continuous mother-infant contact during sleep.[20] Primate researchers have found that disrupting this intimate nighttime contact can quickly prove disastrous.

---

* There's speculation that underreporting of SIDS could contribute to the lower rates in certain areas of Japan,[21] but this would not significantly affect the rates overall.

In one study using rhesus monkeys who had a mechanical "mother surrogate," researchers cooled down the mother's temperature at night, which caused the infant monkeys to move away from her and sleep alone. After two weeks, one infant died. The necropsy found nothing wrong other than dehydration. The veterinarian who performed the necropsy made an off-hand comment that the little monkey had actually died of a "broken heart."[22]

Fortunately human infants don't suffer such a swift demise when left to sleep alone. But with what we've learned from science in recent years, it's little wonder that our babies absolutely yearn for physical contact with a caring adult throughout the night. And it's not surprising that they would react strongly—with cries and often screams—when a separation is forced on them, leaving them frighteningly devoid of one of their basic survival needs.

It Just Feels Right

Just as babies are born with an innate need and desire to be close to their parents day and night, many parents—particularly mothers—have this same desire. A mother trying to do the "right" thing may place her newborn into a bassinet or crib to sleep and go off to her own bed. Often what she feels is excruciating emptiness.

This is partly because the hormonal changes that take place during labor and immediately after delivery create a strong drive for remaining connected with the baby. Prolactin and oxytocin, both of which continue to be secreted at high levels during breast-feeding, make mothers yearn for closeness and intimacy, for touching, fondling, holding, protecting. Separation from the baby triggers natural feelings that "something is not right."[23] These feelings are also intense in women who don't breast-feed, but the hormonal changes that occur with breast-feeding can deepen them.

Parents who are able to listen to their hearts instead of what they've been brought up to assume about solitary infant sleep usually stumble onto a magnificent discovery: Nothing feels as good, or as right, as sleeping beside their baby or young child. No wonder 98 percent of the family bed parents we interviewed and heard from via our extensive questionnaire said they would have their child sleep in the family bed again in a heartbeat! (See "About Our Questionnaires/Interviews," page 197, for more about this research.)

"We both love to be able to open our eyes and see our precious little girl sleeping, and we both love to be able to cuddle with her at any time," says Lora, mother of a sixteen-month-old girl. "I love the reassurance of being able to reach over and touch her and feel her breathing. There is nothing more relaxing and sweet than nursing a baby to sleep and then snuggling with her while she is sleeping."

Working parents also find great joy in the family bed. Sleeping close to their children helps make up for the time they spend away. "Working outside the home is one of the main reasons we fell into co-sleeping," says Suzy, mother of two boys. "This is my time to play catch-up from the day with both my husband and child. This way we're all together, sharing our physical space and events of the day. . . . It feels so good."

Crib Notes

Cozy and beneficial as the family bed can be, and as much as we recommend it, it's not for everyone.

Parents who can't guarantee a safe and sober bed setup shouldn't have a family bed (see chapter 3 for essential bed-sharing safety tips). Likewise when one or both parents are dead set against the family bed, or have tried it but ended up even more sleep deprived because of an extremely mobile infant. Being an overtired, resentful, and potentially angry parent does an infant no favors.

A man once approached us with a dilemma: He liked the idea of the family bed, but the reality was that when he and his wife tried it a few times, he couldn't stand the slurps and gurgles and movements of their baby. "I love him, but when he's in bed with us, I feel like I'm sleeping with the enemy," he said. "The next day I'm worn out and not very patient with him." For this family, letting the baby sleep in his crib made the most sense. With dad happier and relaxed, life was better for everyone.

Fortunately for babies, most parents who give themselves a chance make excellent family bedders. After all, nothing could be more natural.

One point we want to stress: If a child is treated with love and respect at bedtime, and throughout the night if she needs you, she can be content in a crib and grow up to be happy and emotionally healthy. (After all, most of us did—the huge increase in psychoanalysts in the last couple of generations notwithstanding.) In rare cases some babies even seem to prefer sleeping alone. By no means do we condemn caring parents who respect their children's needs at bedtime—wherever they may have chosen to let them sleep—and who give them the comfort and love their children crave, both day and night.

The Late-Night, Self-Serve Buffet (and Other Benefits of Being a Family Bed Baby)

Sleeping with baby was designed by evolution to go hand-in-hand with breast-feeding. If you're breast-feeding your baby, you'll know by now that babies who breast-feed need to do it fairly frequently. That's because human breast milk, while ideally suited to a baby's nutritional needs, is low in fat and protein.[24] Babies who breast-feed get hungry and eat more often than their bottle-fed counterparts.

At night, if your baby sleeps in her own room and needs to eat, she first has to wake up enough to cry to get your attention. Then you have to get out of your warm bed, trudge to the baby's room, nurse her (or bring her to her mom to nurse if you're not designed with the appropriate equipment), get her back to her crib, calm her, go back to your room, and try to fall asleep again before she awakens for more. Parents of bottle-fed babies go through a similar routine. It's usually not as frequent, but it involves things like pouring formula and warming bottles, so it's not exactly a walk in the park either.

The family bed provides a delectably simple alternative. Your baby is hungry. She wakes up, but not fully, finds her mom's breast, perhaps with a little help from her barely awake mother if she's too young to move much. She drinks and drifts back to sleep, as does mom. It's essentially a self-serve wet bar, and it's so simple and easy it's almost too good to be true. No wonder so many breast-fed babies—in one study, 80 percent[25]—end up in the family bed, even if things didn't start that way.

"If I would have had to leave our cozy warm bed to tear to another room, pick up our scared, hungry baby, sit in the cold while he snuggled into me, then return to a now-cold bed, I would probably have been a raving lunatic within days," says Debbie, mother of a two-year-old boy. "As it was, I got plenty of sleep (as did my husband)."

It turns out that if your baby is in bed with you, she'll likely breast-feed more frequently and for longer bouts. This helps with your baby's healthy weight gain and with immune defense against disease, thanks to the antibodies passed on from the mother.[26]

A bonus for parents: Studies show that breast-feeding moms who co-sleep evaluate their sleep more positively than those whose infants are in other rooms.[27] Mothers actually sleep somewhat better, and longer, when their babies are with them.[28] It seems this extra breast-feeding does little to disrupt their sleep. "She didn't have to cry," says Sue, about the first of four children (now grown) who ended up in the family bed. "She would just 'say' that she needed to nurse. I would roll over and lift up my nightshirt. She would latch on, and I was able to enjoy her or, if I preferred, go back to sleep."

Says Marie, a new mom who brought her baby to bed within days: "I could just lie on my side for her to latch on, then just go back to sleep. . . . I had been prepared to become the walking zombie I had heard all new mothers were, [but] I felt great."

A little good nighttime sleep can go a long way when it comes to your daytime parenting. If you're well rested, chances are it will make being a parent easier. As Kathryn, a mother of an eighteen-month-old family bed boy says, "I sleep better. And I am nicer because of it."

A good night's sleep is one reason so many working parents share a bed with their babies. Mom Megan had to return to work when her first child was just six weeks old. "The only way I got enough sleep was to keep him in bed with me so I could sleep while nursing," she says.

The convenience of the family bed also extends to bottle-fed babies, since the baby barely has to awaken to get your attention. Plus, all those trips to the baby's room, and to late-night TV-land if your child doesn't go back to sleep, go by the wayside. If you have a bottle-warmer by the bed, you're all set. "I just pre-made the bottles and kept them next to the bed. [When the baby woke up], I rolled over, got a bottle, fed him, and pretty much went back to sleep," says Michelle, mother of two boys.

A related advantage of the family bed: Studies show co-sleeping babies cry less at night.[29] They don't need to wail to get your attention. Often, they don't cry at all. They just fidget. Or gurgle. Or give a request like "Ehhh ehhhh!" Since you're right there, you can respond before the crying sets in.

Family bed dads often find it easy and enjoyable to get in on whatever comforting action might be needed. "It's personally gratifying to help our baby resettle himself," says John, father of an eight-month-old boy. "Although I can't nurse him back to sleep, I can rub his tummy and sing to him. Usually the fear of having to listen to Daddy's off-key warbling is enough to put him right back to sleep."

Other important "perks" of the family bed:

- Bed-sharing parents are able to immediately help if their infant chokes, cries, has trouble breathing because of a cold, or needs to be warmer or cooler. As you've already seen, this can be a lifesaver.

- Children with disabilities can have a great advantage in the family bed: Their parents can help them in a split second if needed. Jake, who has severe and multiple disabilities from a rare chromosome disorder, has very low muscle tone in his upper body. Breathing is always a concern for his parents, as are seizures. But his parents don't lose sleep over potential problems at night, because they're an arm's reach away. "Some of our sense of security comes from knowing he's sleeping safe and sound," says his mother, Penny.

  In addition, we know of several cases where a disabled child's physical closeness with co-sleeping parents has led to an emotional closeness that make days and nights much easier than they may have otherwise been. In Jake's case, even though he is four years old and can't sit up on his own or speak because of his disabilities, his mother says, "He is a happy little kid, full of grins and giggles, with mischief in his eyes. I'm sure that some of his sense of emotional security comes from getting plenty of physical reinforcement at night."

• Co-sleeping parents of adopted and foster babies say the children thrive when they sleep next to them. "Co-sleeping can make a difference, even in the short-term. Babies we've had for even a few days or weeks have shown definite improvement," says one of many co-sleeping adoptive and foster parents we know. (She shall remain nameless because case workers don't always take kindly to co-sleeping.)

• Single parents often credit the family bed with their very survival in the early months. "If I had to get up and go to a crying baby several times a night, and then function without a partner the next day and night, and do the same night after night, I'd collapse," says Emily, mother of a four-month-old boy.

• Parents of twins also often credit co-sleeping with saving their sanity. "When they were in their own room, one would wake up and cry and he'd wake his brother up, and they'd both be bawling for me. I had to run into their nursery out of a deep sleep, and I thought I was going to have a heart attack some nights trying to calm them both down," says Sylvia, mother of three-year-old twins. "When we switched to co-sleeping, it was vastly easier. They didn't wake each other (or barely me) when they woke up hungry. Much more peaceful, except for me ending up with four little feet in my ribs at times!"

• Parents of all co-sleeping children are right there for a variety of nonmedical emergencies, from home intrusion to fires and natural disasters. (Not that you'll be able to protect your child forever, but in those early months and years, the added protection of the family bed can be invaluable.)

Paula, who has two girls, tells this alarming story: "Once someone broke into the house while the girls and I were home and my husband at work. We had all just climbed into our bed upstairs when the alarm started to go off. I went downstairs to see why and realized that burglars were in the office downstairs stealing computer equipment. I ran upstairs and called the police and told the girls to get in my closet and wait there until the police came. Luckily, we were all fine and the burglars took what they wanted and left, but I just couldn't imagine how I would have panicked if the girls had been downstairs by themselves in their own rooms, alone and close to the burglars."

After the Loma Prieta earthquake in 1989, many Northern California babies found themselves in a completely new environment: their parents' beds. Robert, of San Francisco, was among the parents who decided that the crib was too far away and that the safest place for his child was between him and his wife.

What started as disaster preparedness ended up as a way of life. Even when the threat of aftershocks was long gone, the couple kept their daughter beside them at night. "We felt connected to our baby and found it convenient," Robert says. Besides, their daughter seemed to love it as much as they did. Their third child is now enjoying the comforts of the family bed.

Surrogate Security

The image of a young child sucking her thumb and/or clutching a threadbare security blanket or favorite stuffed animal is ubiquitous in our culture. Many view these activities as a normal, healthy part of development.

"Often, such objects can seem more important to the anxious child than the presence of the mother herself," notes a study from the Case Western Reserve University School of Medicine.[30]

But researchers are discovering a fascinating phenomenon about the use of these "transitional" objects: When a child routinely goes to sleep in the presence of an adult, or with an adult holding her, it's extremely rare to find thumb sucking or attachment to security objects.[31,32,33] "The transitional object is far from a universal event in the course of normal child development," notes the Case Western study.

In one study, 96 percent of a group of thumb-sucking children between the ages of one and seven years had been left alone to fall asleep as infants. In stark contrast, there were no thumb suckers among a large group of children who had physical contact with an adult while falling asleep.[34]

Another study, of children three to five years old, showed that solitary sleepers were far more likely to use a security object than co-sleepers. The researchers concluded that children use security objects as substitutes for nighttime human touch.[35]

The notion that infants should learn to comfort themselves when possible, with objects replacing parents, is a popular one in our culture. Richard Ferber, M.D., director of the Center for Pediatric Sleep at Children's Hospital in Boston, even goes so far as to advise parents whose children don't already have a security object (which he calls a "special toy") to offer their children some viable candidates for this role. "It will give him a feeling of having a little control over his world because he may have the toy or blanket with him whenever he wants, which he cannot expect from you," he writes in his best-selling sleep-training book, *Solve Your Child's Sleep Problems*.[36]

But what do children learn from this? "One would wonder whether these child-rearing practices may be teaching children not to rely on other people as a way of handling stress, but to rely on objects for comfort," conclude Abraham Wolf, Ph.D., and Betsy Lozoff, M.D., in a groundbreaking study on transitional objects.[37]

That would be sad. But it may be true. It certainly is food for thought. Just how much of our feverish consumer culture may have had its start with a baby viewing "things" as paramount, people as unavailable?

They Turn Out Terrific

You're there for your baby when she needs you. You give her countless hours more tender snuggles, and more affection than if she were left alone to sleep. If she wakes up at night, all she has to do is see you or reach out and touch you to feel the world is safe and right.

As she grows older, she doesn't have to face the monsters alone. If she has a nightmare, she awakens to the comforting reality of her loving parents. When she can talk, she will—a great deal, if typical, before falling asleep: Family bed children tend to open up before sleep slips into them. Through their pre-sleep conversations and stories, you can get to know a family bed child on a level you might not otherwise. In the words of Thomas Anders, M.D., a professor of psychiatry at the University of California, Davis, School of Medicine, and director of the school's infant and family sleep laboratory: "Co-sleeping encourages family closeness."[38]

The results of our extensive questionnaire and interviews of 250 family bed parents confirmed this deep family bond. An overwhelming number of respondents said they feel closer to their children, and that their children feel closer to them, at least in part because of the family bed. (We're not saying the family bed is the guaranteed way to get a happy kid. While the family bed can help temper a more difficult temperament, it won't turn a spirited child into Miss Mellow. And it certainly doesn't cancel out the effects of less positive family dynamics.) The vast majority of the family bed graduates (mostly young adults) we heard from during our research agreed they have an incredibly close relationship with their parents and siblings (see chapter 8 for some of their reminiscences).

Rachel, twenty-two, is among the preponderance of family bed graduates who feel extraordinarily close to their families. She believes her family's sleeping situation was at the core of their strong and healthy attachment. "I remember feeling like every night was a slumber party for a time," she says. "My older sister was sleeping in a palette next to my parents' bed, my brother and I were sleeping in or near the bed. . . . We were all very close, both spatially and emotionally, and we have carried that closeness throughout our lives."

Our culture is entering a new era in its views on co-sleeping, thanks in part to research that knocks flat the myths and ideas of the past decades. For years psychology viewed family bed mothers as emotionally withdrawn from their children—theorizing that they use the family bed to make up for their guilt over their "maternal psychopathology."[39,40] Family bed parents were presumed to be in the throes of a bad marriage, and their children were seen as overly needy, perhaps even seeking to displace the parent of the same sex.[41] These erroneous ideas, when combined with the already-taboo nature of co-sleeping in our society, didn't do much for the family bed's image.

More recent psychological research, to the contrary, underscores what co-sleeping families have been saying the whole time: It's really OK to have a family bed—in fact, in most cases, it's optimal.

It turns out that young children who co-sleep in a loving environment actually become better adjusted adults than those who sleep alone, without parental contact.[42] Some of the findings:

- Children who never slept in their parents' beds were harder to control, less happy, had more tantrums, handled stress less well, and were more fearful than routinely co-sleeping children.[43]
- Co-sleepers showed a feeling of general satisfaction with life.[44]
- Children who didn't co-sleep end up getting more professional help with emotional and behavioral problems than co-sleepers.[45]
- Boys who slept in the family bed had increased self-esteem and less guilt and anxiety. Girls had more comfort with physical contact and affection.[46]
- Children who had co-slept felt they weren't as prone to peer pressure as others their age.[47]

It's long been an accepted tenet of psychology that children who have responsive, sensitive, accessible parents are much more likely to be happier later in life.[48,49] It should come as no surprise, then, that children whose parents are there for them day and night turn out so well.

A Declaration of Independence

One of the most important findings of this new co-sleeping research may help put an end to the pervasive question of the independence of family bed children. It's an understandable concern. Most of us grew up with the notion that independence is imperative, and the sooner we learn it, the better. The earliest benchmark of this cultural ideal: a baby in a separate crib or bed, in a separate room.

Just a glimpse at the history of the United States should have been enough to put this myth to rest a long time ago. As one study on co-sleeping concludes: "If leaving children to fall asleep alone truly fosters independence, it is perhaps surprising that during historical periods in the U.S. in which 'independence' was most vividly demonstrated, such as the colonial period, or the westward movement, children were not likely to fall asleep alone."[50]

But since history lessons usually focus on big battles, not little children, this isn't the kind of tidbit we learn in school. The family bed and independence are usually seen as such opposing forces that they rarely even get to occupy space in the same sentence—unless that sentence is something along the lines of: "How on earth can your child learn independence when she's in the family bed?" (Most family bed parents are well acquainted with this question.)

But this is like saying that by putting a baby in diapers, she'll be in diapers throughout her life, or that by using a stroller or carrying her, she'll never learn to walk. Children, given time to learn to trust those around them, and thus learn that their own feelings and needs are legitimate, will develop a true, enduring sense of independence.

Thomas Lewis, M.D., wrote eloquently about the subject in his acclaimed book, A General Theory of Love: "Too often, Americans think that self-rule can be foisted on someone in the way a traveler thrusts a bag at a bellhop: Compel children to do it alone, and they'll learn how; Do it with them and spawn a tentacled monster that knows only how to cling.... Independence emerges naturally not from frustrating and discouraging dependence, but from satiating dependence. Children rely heavily on parents, to be sure. And when they are done depending, they move on—to their own beds, houses, and lives."[51]

As evidence about the benefits of co-sleeping accumulates, it's becoming increasingly common to find positive references like this about the independence of family bed children. This is a refreshing change from the contents of the books that hooked our culture for the last few decades.

Millions of parents have read—and been influenced by—what renowned children's sleep expert Richard Ferber, M.D., wrote about independence in his best-selling book, *Solve Your Child's Sleep Problems.* "Although taking your child into bed with you for a night or two may be reasonable if he is ill or upset about something, for the most part this is not a good idea. . . . Sleeping alone is an important part of his learning to be able to separate from you without anxiety and to see himself as an independent individual."[52]

But surprisingly, these words no longer reflect how Dr. Ferber feels. "I wish I hadn't written those sentences," he said in a 1999 article in *The New Yorker* magazine. "That came out of some of the existing literature. It is a blanket statement that is just not right."[53] This was a courageous revelation coming from a man whose very name is synonymous with solitary sleep.

In fact, there's practically no scientific evidence to support any benefit of solitary infant sleep—particularly in matters of independence. Rather, there's a wealth of new research to the contrary:

- Solitary sleepers have actually been found to be more dependent on their parents than co-sleepers.[54]

- Co-sleeping boys ages three and older were shown to have no greater difficulty separating from one or both parents than solitary sleeping boys. (In this study, girls were not observed for this trait.)[55]
- The majority of family bed graduates consider themselves more independent than their peers.[56]

Many family bed "graduates" who responded to our question-naire expounded passionately about the relationship between their independence, their close family bond, and the family bed. A medical student at the University of California, Los Angeles, who slept with her parents until she was four, and had the freedom to come and go whenever she liked after that, has this to say about the nature of her independence:

"I definitely am more independent and self-directed than my peers.... I think that my ability to strike out on my own was very much influenced by the confidence and security I had in my parents' love.... I think I'm closer to my parents because I knew that they were always accessible to me and that I was their number one priority, and I think that the family bed was one of the ways they showed me that.... I knew I always could count on my parents to be there when I needed them and not just between the hours of 8:00 A.M. and 10:00 P.M."

The mother of a ten-year-old British Columbia boy who slept in the family bed until he was five says people used to interrogate her about the issue of independence: "But any family and friends who know our son don't question us on the family bed making kids dependent anymore. He is just such proof positive that the opposite is true!"

The boy, who goes by the name L.A., agrees with his mom that he's very independent. But at the same time, he has a soft spot for his parents. He says he thinks the family bed helped make his family very close. Comparing himself with his peers, L.A. says, "I'm not as whiny, and I love my parents more. (My friend tells his parents to shut up!) And I trust my parents more. I felt safer and happier in the family bed. I felt like I was more loved."

This boy doesn't need to know the science behind why he felt this way or why he turned out as he did. These days he's more interested in hockey and hanging out with his friends. But his advice for new parents reflects everything science has recently discovered about the incredible benefits of co-sleeping: "Let your baby sleep in the bed. You'll thank yourself later," he says. "And your baby will thank you, too."

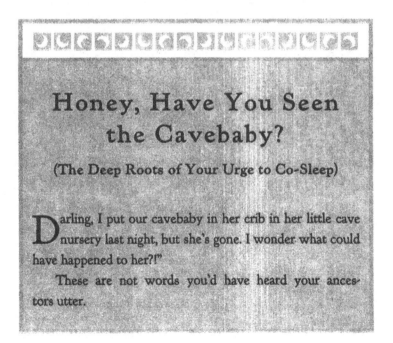

Honey, Have You Seen the Cavebaby?

(The Deep Roots of Your Urge to Co-Sleep)

Darling, I put our cavebaby in her crib in her little cave nursery last night, but she's gone. I wonder what could have happened to her?!"

These are not words you'd have heard your ancestors utter.

If they had, you probably wouldn't be here right now.

Back in the days of humankind's infancy, babies slept snuggled with a parent or caretaker (Fred and Wilma Flintstone's nursery for Pebbles notwithstanding). It was a saber-toothed-eat-man world out there, and sleeping close upped the chances of survival of the next generation. "An infant sleeping alone, even among human hunter-gatherers, would be subject to almost certain death by predation," explains renowned anthropologist Melvin Konner.[57]

In addition to not letting your offspring become dinner (not a big issue today, perhaps), the benefits of co-sleeping were vast enough that it has been the sleeping style of choice for millions of years. Certainly in Western cultures, there's evidence of cradles, boards, and other separate sleeping devices for the last two thousand years or so, but co-sleeping was the norm in our culture all the way up until the last century or two.[58] (And it is still the norm in most other cultures. For more on this, see "Around the World in Forty Winks," page 137.)

No one knows for certain exactly what caused the downfall of co-sleeping in the West, but it was probably a combination of several factors:

• For centuries, and well into the 1800s, it was common knowledge that some destitute mothers smothered their babies in bed and claimed it was an accident. In many areas, it became illegal to sleep with a baby or young child (see "Under Penalty of Death or Vegetables," page 64, for more about this).

- During the 1700s and 1800s, doctors began to believe that co-sleeping wasn't as hygienic as separate sleeping. Ads for twin beds even suggested that breathing someone else's breath was harmful.[59]

- English nannies became very powerful influences in families in the 1800s, imposing strict eating and sleeping regimens for babies and children.[60]

- The Industrial Revolution created major changes in families, which shifted from extended families to smaller, nuclear families. Mothers, lacking help from other relatives, felt it essential to foster their babies' independence as early as possible.[61]

- Physical separation from children, especially during sleep, was deemed to increase a father's ability to display moral authority and to dispense religious training.[62]

- Nineteenth-century parents were told by doctors that crying was actually good for a baby, which made it easier for parents to let them sleep (and cry) alone.[63]

The early 1900s marked the end of co-sleeping being fairly acceptable, with parenting manuals and popular magazines dispensing advice against letting a baby sleep with a parent.[64,65]

While it may seem like solitary infant sleep has been

around for a long time, the current popularity of making infants sleep alone is the exception—perhaps even just a reversible blip—in a very long history of human sleep.

We hope the time has come for babies to take back the night.

2.

Tales from the Crib
How a Bunch of
Little Babies Got Out

The first night Chris, a thirty-eight-year-old chef, squeezed his 220-pound body into the crib where his baby was crying was the first night anyone in the house got a good night's sleep since little Jenny was born.

It was a desperate move—one that could be made only by a sleep-deprived parent with gray pillows for eyes and an unsettling queasiness from not having slept more than two hours in a row for weeks. The pain of the crib slats pressing into his head and his back was nothing compared with the agony of exhaustion. Since Jenny seemed so content to have someone near her as she slept, Chris came to use this big-bear-in-a-little-cage technique several more times in the following weeks.

Then late one night, the bottom fell right out from under his new-found survival skill, and he and Jenny went tumbling to the floor.

Luckily, no one was hurt. But it was a rude awakening, in more than one sense. "We finally realized the crib was not for our baby; she needed to be with us," he says. Ignoring the mounds of advice they'd heard against taking a baby into bed, Chris and his wife brought Jenny to sleep beside them. They snuggled close and slept deeply until morning. They kept this up every night for two years, until Jenny decided to start sleeping in her own bed. "Letting her sleep in our bed was wonderful—the best thing in the world at that time for Jenny, and for us," says Chris.

Little Jenny is among a steadily growing cadre of babies who have persuaded their parents that life in a crib is not always a bed of roses. In the last several years, babies in our culture have been making their way to their parents' beds in unprecedented numbers. Although most parents in the United States don't readily admit sharing their bed with their baby, most do, at least some of the time. (For more on this, see "Will the Real Family Bedders Please Stand Up," page 160.)

"It's becoming less taboo, more acceptable, to bring your baby to bed, and this is extremely important—babies need someone beside them at night," says James McKenna, Ph.D., co-sleeping researcher and anthropology professor at the University of Notre Dame.

The skyrocketing popularity of breast-feeding has been the driving force behind the exodus from crib to parental bed: Sixty-four percent of all new mothers in the United States nurse their infants, at least very early on. There was a 21-percent increase in breast-feeding during the 1990s,[1] and the rate shows no signs of slowing in the beginning of the new century. Nursing babies need to drink more frequently than formula-fed babies. Many a tired new mother has found that taking the baby into bed with her makes it much easier to give the baby night feedings. In fact, 80 percent of breast-fed babies end up in the family bed for at least some of their young lives, according to one study.[2]

With more parents inviting their infants into bed, the stigma of co-sleeping is beginning to lift, although not nearly fast enough for some parents. (If critics are getting you down, see chapter 6 for ideas on how to cope with criticism.) More parenting books and articles refer to the family bed in positive—or at least not entirely negative—terms. Increasingly, psychological research is revealing the great benefits of co-sleeping. With all this, parents who may have been closet co-sleepers in the past are now more likely to share information about their sleep setup with other parents.

"With my first child, I was so ashamed. I thought no one else was doing this, so I kept it a secret. I thought I was all alone," says Ellen, mother of four children from eighteen years to eighteen months. "Now it's like, hey, sure our baby's in the bed. Where else would he be? Crying alone in his crib?"

A backlash against decades of cry-it-out sleep training is emerging as another reason so many babies are waving bye-bye to their cribs (see pages 93–104 for more on these sleep-training methods). "There was no way I was going to do what my parents did to me, making my baby cry all alone in a crib," says Rachel, mother of three young boys. "I have a vague memory of this from when I was two, and it's been with me all these years:

"I was standing there begging my mama to come to the crib for one more hug, crying and crying from my heart when she wouldn't even open the door of the nursery, and finally becoming so exhausted that I fell asleep," she recalls. "She told me just the other day it broke her heart to let me cry, but that's the way things were done back then. I understand that, but, well, that's not how they're done now, at least by me."

Our parenting culture seems to be evolving toward a kinder and gentler one. Parents are becoming more inclined to listen to the needs of their babies and the needs of their own hearts, rather than the mandates of a crib culture. More parents are ignoring the well-decorated bassinet or crib and settling joyously into their bed with their newborn.

"My baby spent nine months inside my body," says mom Brigitte. "To suddenly rip him away from the closeness of my body seemed cruel." (She says her boy's great-grandmother bought his crib and "is horrified that it simply sits there.")

Surprisingly to many, mothers don't have the corner on the market when it comes to this deep desire to sleep near their babies. Many fathers are just as attached.

"I have always depended on the fact that at any time I could just open my eyes and see how my little girl was doing," says Jeff, father of two-year-old Rhanna. "I don't think I would have gotten any sleep at all if I had to get up out of bed to see her in the middle of the night. I would miss her too much."

In another new family, mom Caitlan says her husband was even more likely than she to want their baby in their bed. "We had a crib in our bedroom and once in a while I would put her in it, but my husband would usually take her out and say she couldn't sleep in there all by herself. It was fine with me. . . . We wanted to be close to her; we were just so in love with her."

While more parents these days are opting for a family

bed on their own, the majority of parents still seem to end up bringing their infant to bed because of the baby's "wake-up call." The coaxing from the crib comes in many forms. Occasionally it makes parents laugh, sometimes it makes them cry, and more often than not, it gives them dark circles under their eyes.

If these babies could talk, they'd have some grand tales to tell about their journey from crib to bed. But since they can't generally speak more than a few words, and most of those aren't optimal for storytelling, we relied on their parents to tell their stories.

We now have the pleasure of bringing you the true tales of how a multitude of little munchkins ended up happily snuggled next to their favorite people in the world.

Tears on My Pillow (and My Floor, and the Crib . . .)

One-year-old Linn never liked his crib. "He cried and cried, never slept," says Sam, his mother. "Many, many nights, I slept on the floor in his room, holding his hand, crying. I was exhausted, miserable."

One night, on the brink of collapse, Sam brought Linn into bed with her and her husband. The result? "Oooh, heaven," she says. "He slept. He quit crying. He was wonderful! I slept. My misery left." Ten years later, Linn's three younger siblings have all enjoyed the comforts of the family bed.

Good Nights

There's nothing as convincing as a baby's tears. It's hard to ignore a baby crying in a crib, even though many an advice book has tried—successfully—to get parents to do just that.

Some babies are so unhappy in a crib that they can persuade even the most steadfast crib supporter that a change of venue is in order: "Before Ginnie was born, I thought people with kids in their beds must be pretty strange. Then the crying began, and the only way she would ever calmly fall asleep was beside me, in bed," says her mom. "I decided I was wrong about those people with kids in their beds."

It's important to realize that babies who are unhappy in their cribs aren't "bad" sleepers, aren't spoiled, and aren't manipulating. What they are is good at communicating their deepest baby needs, needs that have been etched into our genes for millions of years—needs that helped babies survive long ago, when solitary babies made good meals for hungry creatures lurking nearby.

Yet when a baby expresses this built-in need to sleep beside a parent or grandparent rather than alone in a crib, we're often surprised. "I had no idea that babies could have such a strong opinion on sleeping arrangements at that young an age!" says Laura, whose three-week-old daughter would cry every time mom and dad tried to get her near a bassinet when sleeping at her great-grandparents' house. (Luckily, her girl was always a family bedder when in her own home.)

Parents who try the family bed after weeks or months of dealing with a child who cries when left alone to sleep are often especially jubilant about the results. It's striking how frequently these parents use words like "miracle" and "slept through the night" when describing their child's first encounter with the family bed:

- "Out of desperation, I brought him to bed with us. It was an absolute miracle! He slept all night," says Kelly of her son, who, at eighteen months, had been waking up unhappy in his crib a few times a night.

- "The very first night [in the family bed], she slept the entire night... we had stumbled on a miracle! From that very first night, she slept through the night," says Julie, mother of four children ages fourteen to three, of the time when her eldest, sleepless daughter was twenty months old. (All of Julie's subsequent children were welcome into the bed from the beginning.)

- "We all stopped crying and started sleeping. It was a real miracle," says Maddy, whose son's sleepless nights had just about the whole family in tears until they discovered the family bed when he was eleven months old.

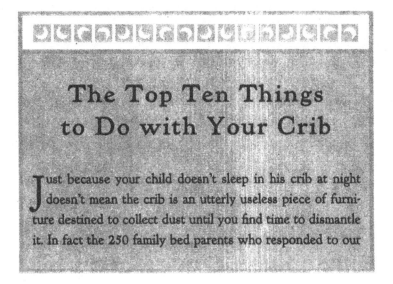

The Top Ten Things
to Do with Your Crib

Just because your child doesn't sleep in his crib at night doesn't mean the crib is an utterly useless piece of furniture destined to collect dust until you find time to dismantle it. In fact the 250 family bed parents who responded to our questionnaire and interviewed with us had some very creative uses for their cribs. Here are the ten most common ways they put their cribs to work:

1. Safe napping space for the baby/good sidecar for bed when side is removed

2. Very spacious laundry basket

3. Super deluxe changing table

4. Fanciest cat bed on the block

5. Safe baby play area when parent has to run to bathroom

6. Bed for stuffed animals

7. Jail for stuffed animals gone horribly wrong (also, cage for children playing Hansel and Gretel, prison for evil cowboys, etc.)

8. Attractive decoration in a precious, pricey, unused room

9. Baby gift holder/cello holder/toy box/holder of anything that would otherwise clutter the rest of the house

10. Decoy for people who don't need to know that the baby really sleeps in the family bed

Rock Around the Clock

Baby Julie kissed her crib good-bye via a technique many babies have used: the desire for eternal rocking. Julie's mother, Cheryl, would rock in her new rocker for an hour or two until Julie drifted off. Then she'd carefully place Julie in her crib and tiptoe to her own bed to try to get a couple of hours of sleep before Julie woke up again. An hour or two later, when Julie awoke, it was back to the rocker routine. This went on a few times every night, and Cheryl felt like she was going to go off her rocker, in more ways than one.

Cheryl and her husband had tried different techniques to get Julie to be a better sleeper. They'd even tried a "cry-it-out" sleep-training method for three weeks when Julie was seven months old, but she woke up every hour, crying for twenty minutes each time. "It was a disaster," says Cheryl.

Cheryl had heard about the family bed when Julie was only two months old; but since her husband was against it, she gave up on the idea. Now, with Julie close to a year, Cheryl decided that the only way she would survive short of the family bed was to delegate some of her rocking hours to her husband.

It didn't last long. Just a few days after her husband took on the rocking stints, he decided the family bed might be a good option after all. Once Julie adjusted to the bed (Cheryl initially had to "rock" her to sleep at the bed's edge), they all started sleeping well. "She actually slept like a baby," says Cheryl. "What a relief!" Their next two children slept in the family bed from the outset.

Baby Julie was in good company with her need to be "in

arms" (and often "on breast") to fall asleep. It's very common for a baby to crave the touch of a loving parent at night (see chapter 1 for more on the benefits of touch). Rocking chairs are soothing for the baby, and socially acceptable locations for night comforting and nursing in our culture. When used frequently in the wee hours, they're often a springboard to the family bed.

Here's how a few other chair-happy cherubs ended up in the family bed:

- "My baby would sleep in my arms in a chair all night long, but I was getting no sleep," says Marieann. "Everyone said to put him in his crib and let him cry it out. That ripped my heart out, so I sat up rocking him instead. He was six months old when I finally realized that he HAD to come to bed with me. No one had ever offered that solution to the problem." She brought him to bed, and "we both got the much-needed rest we hadn't been getting. It worked out wonderfully from the start."

- "I swore I would never do this, but after two weeks of sleeping in the living room chair, I collapsed into bed with my baby," says Katharine. "[It was] much better...a true blessing!"

- "She just wanted to nurse all night long. We'd sit in the chair, she'd drink drink drink, as they say in the opera, then on the way back to the crib, I'd literally be falling asleep while walking," says Carolyn. "One day I walked back to my bed with her and accidentally fell asleep. Lo and behold, we slept all night. It was the beginning of a beautiful relationship."

• "My first child was only days old and was nursing late into the night. I caught myself falling asleep in the chair and was afraid I would drop him," says Jane. "I took him to bed and found out that I did not have to be awake to nurse him! That changed my life."

A Little Night Music

Remarkably, music has been the key to a number of babies leaving the crib.

Five-month-old Taylor convinced her parents about the virtues of the family bed by wearing out their vocal cords. Her mother or father would hold her until she fell asleep, then tiptoe to the nursery to place her in her crib. Inevitably, says her mom, "she would jolt awake from a deep sleep as we crossed through the doorway." (Ahh, baby radar.)

Based on past experience, the only option then would be to croon to Taylor while she lay in her crib. Ten minutes into the act, one or both parents would still be there singing away. Twenty minutes later they'd still be humming and crooning. A half-hour, forty minutes, fifty minutes dragged by, and the singing continued. It generally took an hour or more for Taylor to tire of her troubadors and nod off.

One night, enough was enough. Taylor had slept in bed with her parents at one point in her young life, and everyone had slept well. They knew their next move. That night her parents re-established the family bed, and they, and their vocal cords, now rest comfortably every night.

Little Kevin wound up in the family bed in much the same

way, only he had a specific song he needed night after night: "The Wheels on the Bus." His mother had made up an additional twenty or so choruses ("it took about thirty rounds to get him to sleep," she says), and if she missed one of them, which was all too easy to do in the dark of night when her brain was leaden with fatigue, Kevin would be so distraught she'd have to start all over in order to calm him down.

After months of this, she felt that if she had to sing "Wheels on the Bus" one more time she'd throw herself under one. She had read an article on the family bed and decided to try it. Kevin snuggled next to her and drifted off before the people on the bus even had a chance to go up and down.

And Down Will Come Baby . . .

Little Jenna wasn't wild about sleeping in her crib, but she'd been doing it off and on for eighteen months and was pretty used to it. One night she decided the grass was greener on the other side of the crib rail and tried to get out. But she got stuck halfway in a painful and frightening position. Her body was folded in half, legs out of the crib, head dangling down into the crib. She didn't have the strength or size to move one way or the other.

She cried out, but no one heard her. As luck would have it, the intercom system wasn't working that night.

By the time her mother heard her cries (she doesn't know how long Jenna had been hanging there), Jenna was "very, very upset." Her mother felt terrible, and brought her into her bed. Jenna had no desire to escape from that bed, and she slept beside her parents until she was ready for her own toddler bed.

Many parents end up taking their babies into bed with them because of some kind of scare. When a child's life or well-being is at stake, most parents don't think twice about letting him sleep in their bed.

Justine, mother of three adult children, was seven months pregnant with her first child when a friend's toddler climbed out of his crib one night, slipped, and fell on his head. The little boy suffered permanent brain damage.

"It had a profound effect on me," says Justine, who never let her children spend one night in a crib.

Illness also transports many a baby from crib to family bed. We've heard from several parents who brought their baby to bed because of a fever, ear infection, or bad cold. The illness cleared up, but the baby stayed on.

One evening, LaJuana looked adoringly into her youngest daughter's bassinet and realized with alarm that her daughter wasn't breathing. The frightened mother shook her, and Caitlin resumed breathing. After that Caitlin slept in her parents' bed. LaJuana says she felt much more aware of Caitlin's breathing patterns when she slept right next to her. She was able to help Caitlin re-establish breathing several times in the next few weeks, until Caitlin's apnea disappeared. (If you suspect your child has apnea, see your pediatrician promptly. Don't rely on co-sleeping as the solution.)

Sometimes it's actually a parent's physical problem that catapults a baby from the crib or bassinet into the family bed. Many of the mothers we interviewed had had Caesarean sections or problematic episiotomies and took to co-sleeping because of the pain.

"My daughter would start crying to be fed, and it would take me a couple of minutes just to get to the cradle at the foot of our bed," says Marie, who had a C-section. On the third night of painful visits to the bassinet, Marie brought her baby to her bed. "It was much, much easier."

No matter how they get there, babies who find themselves in bed next to a loving parent are lucky babies indeed. The benefits to both baby and parent are endless, with everyone generally less tired, more content, often extraordinarily happy, and inevitably relieved.

As Wayne, father of three grown family bed children says, "I wonder why we even tried it any other way?" His sentiment echoes through the bedrooms of all those well-rested parents whose babies finally sold them on the family bed.

Money You'll Save with the Family Bed

Go to the home of typical family bed parents, and you'll likely find a lovely nursery, complete with sleepy pastel farm animals, yawning moons, or congenial clowns. While the decor might vary from one nursery to another, there's one striking similarity about these rooms: They're very neat, and very devoid of signs of anyone sleeping there (save the occasional cat reposing languidly in an unused crib).

"It [the nursery] was the worst investment we ever made," says Sabine, mother of two young boys. This sentiment is shared by many family bed parents who didn't realize they'd be family bed parents until their babies talked them into it.

If you're thinking about letting your baby sleep in your bed and you haven't yet invested in a nursery, you're lucky: Cribs, mattresses, bassinets, bedding, nursery decorations, lamps, and their ilk don't come cheap. You can save an average of $1,200—much more if you opted for top-of-the-line items—if you co-sleep. (That figure doesn't include the cost of items you'll still use as a family bedder, such as a chest of drawers, a rocker, and a changing table.)

Of course, saving money shouldn't be the reason behind

a decision to co-sleep. But we figure it can't hurt to add it to the "pro" side when you're trying to weigh your options before spending the big baby bucks. Take it from these parents, who laid out a sizeable chunk of change for baby stuff they never used:

$$$$ "We have a very nice crib with a very expensive mattress. It was the item I fixated on during my pregnancy. I couldn't sleep for weeks worrying that we would have the baby and no place for it to sleep. Finally, four months before I was due, we got a crib and I rested easier. I also got 100-percent cotton sheets and the recommended two waterproof mattress covers." Now? The cat sleeps in it.

—DELLA, MOM OF A TWO-YEAR-OLD GIRL

$$$$ "We spent $1,900 on a fancy, gorgeous crib setup. It holds blankets and stuffed animals today. Our son loves to jump in and play in it for five minutes or so a week."

—COURAGE, MOM OF A TWO-YEAR-OLD BOY

$$$$ "Every time I look at that empty nursery, I don't even see the nursery. I see the refrigerator and stove we could have bought with the money we spent on it. If only we'd known!"

—DIANA, MOTHER OF TWO BOYS

3.

Practicing Safe Sleep

Essential "Beducation" for Co-Sleepers

ZZZZZZZZZZZZZ z

> *"Mother came to my bed one night bringing my three-week-old baby. She pulled the cover back and told me to get up and hold him while she put rubber sheets on my bed. She explained that he was going to sleep with me.*
>
> *"I begged in vain. I was sure to roll over and crush out his life or break those fragile bones. She wouldn't hear of it, and within minutes the pretty golden baby was lying on his back in the center of my bed, laughing at me.*
>
> *"I lay on the edge of the bed, stiff with fear, and vowed not to sleep all night long . . ."*
>
> —MAYA ANGELOU,
> I KNOW WHY THE CAGED BIRD SINGS

If you're new to the family bed, you probably know how Maya Angelou felt that first night in bed with her baby. You may be anxious you'll roll over and smother your infant. Or you may wake up every fifteen minutes to check if your baby is still breathing.

These fears are understandable. You probably weigh at least fifteen times more than your tiny, sweet-smelling infant. (Proportionally speaking, that's like you sleeping next to a full-grown giraffe.) You may have read harrowing headlines—such as "Sharing Bed with Baby Deadly"—about a study that garnered worldwide attention, despite its faulty methodology and sweeping conclusion (see "The Big, Bad Bed Report" section below). A relative may have even warned you that if you sleep with your baby, you're sure to kill him or at least maim him for life.

We have good news for you.

Sleeping with your baby in your bed is very safe, as long as you follow safe-sleep guidelines. In fact, a safely set up family bed is at least as safe as a safely set up crib. And with all the health benefits babies get from co-sleeping, as we described in chapter 1, it may even be safer.

Keep in mind that nothing—not crib sleeping, not bedsharing, not driving to the supermarket—is 100 percent risk free. But if you follow the safety tips in this chapter and use common sense, you'll be able to provide your baby with one of the safest possible sleep environments.

The Big, Bad Bed Report

A 1999 report from the U.S. Consumer Product Safety Commission recommended that children younger than two years of age never be allowed to sleep in bed with adults.[1]

The report, which garnered "family bed equals death"-type headlines worldwide, also received heavy criticism from the medical community for drawing such a draconian conclusion against co-sleeping, especially in light of what many interpreted as flawed research. Renowned SIDS researcher, Abraham Bergman, M.D., called the report "a classic example of garbage in, garbage out."[2]

If you're interested in learning about the report's numer-ous problems, whether to ease your own mind or assuage a nervous relative, please see appendix A, page 193.

In defense of the CPSC report, it does provide some important data about the nature of infant deaths in adult beds, illuminating hazards such as entrapment or wedging between the mattress and another object, suffocation on water beds, and strangulation in rails or openings on beds that allow a baby's body to pass through while entrapping the head.[3,4] This information has helped pediatricians and family bed researchers provide better guidelines for safer sleep.

Cribs—All They're Cracked Up to Be?

Sleeping in a crib isn't necessarily a panacea for avoiding haz-ardous sleep situations. Tragically, approximately fifty children in the United States die of suffocation or strangulation in cribs each year.[5]

In a review of infant deaths caused by certain types of suf-focation, researchers were surprised at the number of deaths attributed to a wedging incident in a crib: "Few crib deaths were expected, given that the crib regulation has been in effect since 1973," they wrote. The review noted that many of the cribs involved in these deaths may have had structural prob-lems because they were built before strict crib regulations, or because of damage, an improperly fitted mattress, or bad assem-bly. But frighteningly, some cribs involved with mechanical suffocation deaths had no detectable problems.[6]

In addition, faulty manufacture can lead to hazardous cribs: In 2001, one crib company recalled 68,600 cribs because of a defect that could lead to the mattress falling and a baby suffocating.[7]

Even a perfectly set up crib can present hazards. We know several parents who were scared into having a family bed because their children hurt themselves—sometimes severely—when attempting to escape from the crib (see chapter 2 for two of their stories).

More important, the benefits of having your baby near you instead of in a crib in a room down the hall are manifold, as we've already described. Some, such as potential protection from SIDS, may even be lifesaving. Before researchers suggest cribs as the only place for infants to sleep, they need to take a good look at all the evidence.

Bedders Safe, Not Sorry

We know several parents whose children are alive today because they were sleeping in the family bed when a life-threatening problem occurred.

Even though parents may be asleep, it doesn't mean they're unaware. Parents tend to rouse to the rescue when a baby so close is having trouble.

Justine Clegg, midwifery program director at Miami-Dade Community College, tells this story about a family bed baby she helped birth:

When Zachary was about six weeks old, his mother woke up suddenly in the middle of the night and discovered that he wasn't breathing. He was blue. She immediately performed CPR. An ambulance rushed the baby to the hospital, where he was put on a sleep-apnea monitor. Several more times during his hospital stay, he stopped breathing and set off the alarms and had to be resuscitated by the hospital staff.

Both the pediatrician and the baby's mother were sure that if she hadn't been sleeping with him when he had his first episode of sleep apnea, he would have died. Because she slept with him, she was sensitive to his breathing rhythms and woke up when she sensed a change.

Justine reports that Zachary is now "a healthy, happy, handsome, athletic young man of eighteen years."

The Safest Sleep

At first glance, the tips that follow may seem like a lot of work. But setting up a safe family bed isn't difficult at all. It can be as easy as living a healthy lifestyle, putting your mattress on the floor, and keeping blankets and pillows away from baby's head.

A NOTE FROM DR. JAY: *Many family bed parents follow only minimal safety guidelines and never run into trouble. In all my years as a pediatrician, and with all the thousands of little family bedders who have come through my door, there's never even been one close call. And as I mentioned earlier, I've never had a single case of SIDS in my practice. It's not that I'm that good; it's just that the family bed and the huge family relationship it engenders can help make babies so much safer.*

But since your baby's well-being could depend on your following a few simple tips, it's best, by far, to err on the side of caution and create the safest sleep environment possible.

Keep in mind that the younger the baby, the more vulnerable he is. The CPSC study showed that more than three-quarters of overlying deaths (in which a parent inadvertently suffocated a baby by rolling onto the baby while sleeping) occurred in infants younger than three months.[8] While overlying is extremely rare, it does happen. Most parents have a built-in awareness of the baby's presence that prevents them from rolling onto the baby—and wakes them up if they do—but even with this radar, it's important to be extra diligent about hazards that could result in overlying during the early months.

Here then are the very best ways to keep your baby safe and sound in bed:

Crush Your Butt: If you smoke, stop. You stand to harm too many people. If you can't or won't stop, don't smoke anywhere near your baby. Smoking increases the chance of SIDS,[9] whether the baby is in the crib or in the family bed.[10] Research indicates that the greater the exposure to smoke, the greater the risk for SIDS.[11] So family bed children whose parents smoke in the bedroom are at a higher risk.

(A Catch-22: If you're quitting smoking and using a nicotine patch to help you, you're not quite off the hook where your child's safety is concerned; you need to make absolutely sure the patch is on firmly when you go to sleep with your child. Patches have come off parents during sleep and ended up on their children. Since one of these patches has the nicotine equivalent of six to eight cigarettes, it's not the kind of Band-Aid you want your baby to wear.)

Just Say "No": Never sleep with your baby if you (or your partner, if your partner sleeps next to the baby) are under the influence of drugs, alcohol, or prescription medication that makes you groggy or sleepy. You won't be as aware of your infant's presence in bed. For the same reason, try not to be too exhausted when you co-sleep with a tiny baby. (We know this is just about impossible and that most parents fall into co-sleeping because of exhaustion, but since it's a tenet of many co-sleeping experts, we felt we needed to include it here.)

Happy bed tip: A rubber sheet under your baby can mean the difference between a mattress that's rather pungent by the end of your family bed days or one that's like new.

Good Nights

Take Center Stage: While many babies sleep very safely between their parents, some experts say it's safest to have a young baby next to the mother only, because mothers seem to be especially aware of their babies in bed. (The "down" side of this arrangement is that you then have to worry about how to keep the baby on the bed. We have some suggestions later in this chapter.) We've heard from two families where Dad rolled slightly over on the baby only to have Mom wake up and peel him off. In both of those families, the baby ended up sleeping on the side of the bed next to the mother. This sleep setup is especially important in cases where the dads sleep very deeply. As your child gets older, you can allow him to sleep between you.

In truth, most families we've dealt with have slept with the baby between two parents and are just fine. In fact, it seems some of these parents were in more jeopardy than the babies: "Picture this," explains Barbara, mother of four, from Australia. "Mum and Dad on the outer reaches of the bed, each clinging onto a precious half-inch of duvet, while said child lounges horizontally in the middle, head wedged in Mum's back and feet wedged in Dad's posterior. All this in the middle of winter. Who said anything about the child being in danger of falling off?"

Of interest: Most babies, even newborns, aren't the completely helpless creatures many think they are. Even tiny babies have some ability to struggle and squirm and cry in order to get out of potentially dangerous situations. Never throw caution to the wind because of this. But if you're already doing everything as safely as possible, being aware of this might help you be a little more relaxed at bedtime.

Separate the Siblings: If you have an older child in bed with you, be sure to keep an adult between that child and your baby. Children aren't always aware of the presence of a little baby in bed, which could potentially be dangerous.

Get Firm: Sleep on only a firm mattress or futon. Soft or saggy mattresses, featherbeds, sheepskins, and even eggshell foam mattress pads put your young baby at risk of suffocation. Be sure your bottom sheet fits tightly.

And never, ever put your baby down to sleep on a water bed or a couch. Water beds are a major cause of suffocation deaths in babies, and couches have crevices and cushions that can trap a baby's head and also cause suffocation.

The Bigger the Better: The top advice family bedders say they'd give new parents about their bed setup: "Get a king!" They're right. The bigger the bed, the better. As one experienced mom told us: "Even if you start out with just two or three people, you always end up with two Minnie Mouses, one Pikachu, one shark, and a Catdog in there with you." Not only will everyone be much more comfortable with a bigger bed, with fewer little feet in fewer big faces, but it turns out that roomier sleeping arrangements are safer. Crowding into a small bed can be dangerous because the risk of rolling onto your baby is greater. If you already have a small bed, as your baby grows you can get him a twin bed and place it flush against your bed (making sure the beds are at the same level and that there are no crevices or "wells" the baby's face can slip into). The same goes if you are sleeping with more than one child in the bed—in that case, the bigger the extra bed, the better as well.

When Bigger Isn't Better: If you're exceptionally obese, some experts say you should avoid co-sleeping because you may not be as aware of your body's position in relation to your baby. A way around this is to opt for the sidecar method (see next tip for more on this).

Make Like a Motorcycle: If you feel too worried or uncomfortable having your baby in bed beside you, you can use a sidecar setup (kind of like the one in the illustration leading into chapter 8). Commercially available sidecars are often called co-sleepers. These are modified three-sided cribs that attach to the side of the bed and keep babies safely at an arm's reach (thus the name of one popular co-sleeper, the Arm's Reach Co-Sleeper). These provide babies with a safe sleeping area and pretty much prevent a parent from rolling over on the baby, since the baby has his own little environment. Many family bed parents use their baby's otherwise unused crib as a sidecar, lowering one side all the way, putting the crib mattress level with the mattress on the adults' bed, flush against the bed, and making sure there's no space between the crib and the bed.

Or Make a Nest: If you or your spouse are nervous about rolling over on your infant (as we've mentioned, extraordinarily unlikely), you may want to try a "snuggle nest." It's a little pad with protective walls, and its makers advertise it as preventing parent rollover, while still allowing you to snuggle and cuddle with your baby. It's made for the littlest babies, who can't push up or roll over. You can find it (and other similar devices) in popular baby catalogs and stores.

Don't be a Wallflower: Avoid putting your bed or mattress against the wall. Although this may seem like a safe setup so your baby doesn't fall out of bed when sleeping on the outside, babies have suffocated when they've become trapped in a small space between the wall and the bed. If you must have your bed against the wall, make absolutely certain it's flush against the wall. If there's any space at all, firmly pack a towel all the way into it. Check this setup nightly.

How Low Can You Go?: Keeping your bed low to the ground minimizes any falls. The safest way to go is to place your mattress or futon directly on the floor. You may feel a bit like a starving college student, but your interior decorating scheme can take a backseat to your baby's safety for a while. (Just make sure that no one in the bed suffers from allergies to house dust because the closer you get to the ground, the closer you get to dust mites and other allergens. Even if you're not allergic, be sure to keep the floor area as clean and dust-free as you can manage.)

Get Your Head(board) on Straight: If your bed has a headboard and a footboard, make sure they fit tightly, with absolutely no crevices that can trap a small head. If you can fit more than two fingers between the edge of the mattress and the headboard or footboard, your safest bet is to remove them. Some families have gotten around this by placing large, rolled towels into the spaces to completely fill the crevices (checking them nightly), but this isn't foolproof. Fancy headboard designs close to the mattress (such as wrought-iron swirls or horizontal bars) can also be dangerous, so this type of setup is best removed as well.

Be Slat-Happy: If your headboard or footboard has slats, make sure they're no more than 2⅜ inches apart so your baby's head can't slip through. (The same rule goes for cribs.)

Blankets Are Best: Downy duvets and thick comforters may be cozy, but they're also a potential suffocating hazard for infants if they end up over their faces. Light blankets are better, but don't use many. (And never pull the blanket up over the baby's head, of course. Keep it at chest level.) If you're cold, put on more clothes. In colder weather, if you put your baby in a blanket sleeper, make sure he doesn't get overheated. Remember, two or more people sleeping close together can generate a lot of heat. Blanket sleepers were designed with solitary cribbed babies in mind.

Push Away the Pillows: Babies in cribs don't use pillows because they pose a suffocation hazard. Babies in the family bed shouldn't either. To be safe, be sure to keep your own pillows away from your baby's head. It's extremely important to maintain good circulation around your baby's head. For this reason, also be sure all stuffed animals are far from your sleeping baby.

Roll Out the Barrel, Not the Baby:

If your baby sleeps on the side of the bed, as opposed to between parents, make sure he can't fall or roll off the side. One way to do this is with guardrails (also known as bed rails), which are available at most baby stores. Unfortunately, a recent study found that even guardrails are not 100 percent safe for babies, since small babies can potentially roll over into them and get lodged in dangerous positions.

The U.S. Consumer Product Safety Commission is work-ing with the guardrail industry to make guardrails safer. In the meantime, if you use a guardrail, and if there's any space between it and your bed, fill in that space with firmly rolled towels. You may also want to put a firm bolster between your baby and the guardrail so your baby can't have direct contact with the rail.

Make Yours Sunny-Side Up: Always place your baby on his back to sleep, never on his stomach. The face-down position is a major risk factor for SIDS, according to recent statistics.

(The only exception to the no-stomach-sleeping rule is if your pediatrician has diagnosed a medical condition where your baby needs to be placed on his tummy.)

Babyproof Your Boudoir: Even if you're not a co-sleeper, it's a good idea to childproof your bedroom. But if your little one sleeps with you, it's imperative. Check everything from the cords on blinds (making sure they aren't in a "loop" that can become a noose) to wall outlets and window locks.

Contain Your Coif: If your hair is really long, keep it tied. Very long, loose hair can pose a strangulation hazard.

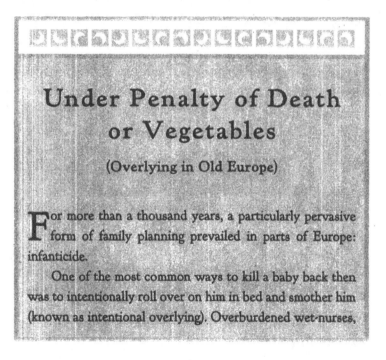

Under Penalty of Death or Vegetables

(Overlying in Old Europe)

For more than a thousand years, a particularly pervasive form of family planning prevailed in parts of Europe: infanticide.

One of the most common ways to kill a baby back then was to intentionally roll over on him in bed and smother him (known as intentional overlying). Overburdened wet-nurses, mothers with children born out of wedlock, and destitute, desperate parents who had too many mouths to feed resorted to overlying frequently enough that as early as A.D. 800, the church and local authorities enacted laws banning babies from parental beds.[12]

Punishment for an intentional overlying death (which was probably impossible to determine unless a parent confessed) varied greatly, depending on the time, the place, and the baby's baptism status. Some mothers and caretakers had to do a mere forty days penance on bread, water, and vegetables, and abstain from intercourse for a year. Some did penance for three years. Others were sentenced to death.[13]

Despite the laws, sharing a bed with a baby remained common. To protect babies in eighteenth-century Italy, nurses were threatened with excommunication if they failed to use a new invention, the *arcutio* (see figure on page 66). This three-foot-long protective wooden device, reminiscent of a pared-down lobster trap, was built to prevent rolling over on a baby in bed.[14]

The *arcutio* came to be highly recommended in England, but it didn't seem to put much of a dent into overlying fatalities: In mid-nineteenth-century London, a time when life was often difficult, coroners' reports show more than 1,100 overlying deaths in a five-year period to be murders, not accidents.[15]

Unfortunately, the legacy of these intentional overlying deaths lives on. Our culture's exaggerated fears of rolling over on a baby in bed stem, in part, from the close association of co-sleeping and infanticide by overlying in bygone centuries.

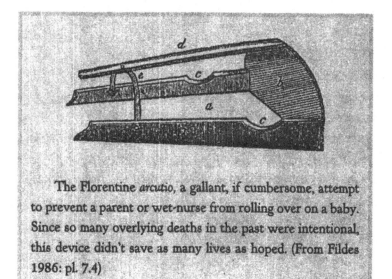

The Florentine *arcutio*, a gallant, if cumbersome, attempt to prevent a parent or wet-nurse from rolling over on a baby. Since so many overlying deaths in the past were intentional, this device didn't save as many lives as hoped. (From Fildes 1986: pl. 7.4)

Naptime Notes

In addition to using the previous safety tips, family bedders have a few special considerations when it comes to naptime. (And also when it comes to leaving your baby alone in bed for a while at night before you go to sleep, or in the morning after you wake up, should you choose not to spend every one of your baby's sleeping minutes with him.)

It's best not to let your baby nap alone on your bed. If you do, be sure to use guardrails and even firm bolsters to keep the baby safely in bed (as discussed in the safety tips in this chapter). Many parents also put extra padding on the floor in case the baby still manages to fall out. A good remedy against your baby plummeting a yard or so down to the floor is to place your mattress directly on the floor, as we also mentioned earlier.

It's important to use a monitor if you're in a different room during these solitary sleep sessions so you can zip in as soon as you hear wriggling. Don't rely on your ears, even if you're in a nearby room. Take it from Suzanne, mother of four children. The family had moved into a new home, and she hadn't yet unpacked the monitor before the five-month-old baby's nap. "I figured he'd be fine as long as we checked every five to ten minutes (he wasn't yet crawling, sitting, or rolling over). Well, one time when I checked, he must have just then wiggled between the bed and the wall. His face was red, not blue, thankfully." The little sounds he was making were inaudible in the next room.

If you opt to sleep with your baby during his naps, you won't have to worry about the dangers of him sleeping solo on your bed. (Plus, you'll be well rested!) But if you have things you need to tend to instead (for instance, the amazing luxuries of going to the bathroom, taking a shower, eating, or spending a little time with your partner), you may want to consider dusting off the crib or bassinet for your baby's nap, if you have these handy. Many family bed parents use their crib only as a safe place for baby to nap, as long as the baby doesn't mind napping there. Some settle the baby into sleep in a sling or in their arms first, and then move the baby into the crib while he's asleep. Again, be sure to use a monitor if you're in a separate room while your baby is in the crib.

A sling or baby carrier are wonderful places for a baby to nap. The rhythm of your body can have a lulling effect on the baby, easing him into a deep, happy sleep. All the extra loving and cuddles can't hurt either. Plus, you have the benefit of knowing he's safe, while you're able to get a few things done. Some parents kick back and watch TV or catch up on e-mail, some take a walk, some even tidy the whole house (sans toxic chemicals) with the baby napping in a sling. "If it wasn't for my babies napping in the sling, my house would have been condemned," says Janice, a busy mom of three. "It was the only time I ever got to clean the place when they were little!"

Safety Tips at a Glance

Here's a handy guide for busy parents who need a quick reminder of the bed-sharing safety tips in this chapter. (We'd call it a crib sheet, but somehow that doesn't seem appropriate.) Be sure to read the whole tips first though, because they cover much more ground.

- If you smoke, stop. If you can't stop, don't do it anywhere near your baby.

- Avoid bed sharing if either partner is drunk, medicated, or using drugs. Exercise caution if a parent is obese.

- Be sure your mattress is very firm and fits the headboard and footboard tightly. Eliminate any crevices or ledges your baby might fall or crawl into. Better yet, put your mattress directly on the floor.

- Avoid putting your bed beside a wall. If you have to do this, be sure to eliminate any crevices that could suffocate your baby.

- Never, ever sleep with a baby on a water bed or sofa.

- If you're uncomfortable sleeping with your baby in your bed, try a specially designed "sidecar."

- Always place your baby on his back to sleep.

- Since mothers may have more awareness of their baby's presence in bed than fathers or siblings, it's safest to put your baby next to the mother only.

- Keep pillows and plush toys away from your baby's head.

- Use only light blankets, no fluffy comforters.

- Babyproof your bedroom.

4.

The Sandman Cometh

Sound Solutions for a
Satisfying Sleep

ZZZZZZZZZZZZZ

The family bed can be blissful. But it's not always a sea of tranquility, with gentle puffs of sweet baby breath caressing your cheek as you sail peacefully down lullaby lane. On some nights, you might awaken to the diaper end of your infant firmly in your face. Or to your baby trying hard to nurse—on your nose—for the fourth time that night. Or to your wide-awake toddler exhorting you to "Get up. Up! Play!" at 3:00 A.M.

Fortunately, a good night's sleep in the family bed isn't just a pipe dream. Many family bed parents and babies sleep very well--much better than they would if they slept separately. And for just about every impediment to a sound snooze, there's a solution—or at least an answer that will help you make it through the night with your sanity intact.

In this chapter we will bring you answers to questions we've been asked by family bed parents about ways to get a better night's sleep. If you have a nighttime woe from the family bed, you'll probably find a solution to it here.

Keep in mind that while difficult nights may seem to last forever, before you know it, it's extremely likely that your little one will be sleeping in her own bed and sleeping well. In the meantime, it helps to remember that a little nurturing nighttime parenting will go a long way toward giving your child the best possible start in life. (We hope this helps make your life a little easier the next time you awaken with your child's toes on your nose.)

Q: All my friends have babies who sleep through the night in their cribs. My seven month old still wakes up two or three or four times a night to nurse. I barely wake up when this happens, and it's no big deal to me, but I feel like we must be doing something wrong. If one more person asks me when my daughter started sleeping through the night, I'm going to flip my lid!

A: First of all, bear in mind that many parents tend to overestimate their children's sleeping prowess. As one San Francisco pediatrician says, "If someone tells you their baby sleeps through the night at a young age and has never come into bed with them, they're probably lying." (See "Sleeping Like a Baby," page 84, for eye-opening facts on sleeping through the night.) You should probably try to hook up with other parents of co-sleeping babies, so you'll be able to get support—and garner realistic expectations—for your situation. (See "Helpful Resources," page 195, for ways to find other co-sleepers.)

Now on to your question of your baby nursing at night: If it's not bothering you, don't change it. Your baby is typical of breast-fed babies, particularly those in the family bed. These children can wake up more frequently to nurse than their cribbed, bottle-fed friends, but it's usually little trouble for mom or baby. This is actually a more natural—and even healthier—situation than the sleep-through-the-night infants have at this age.

Realize that your baby's night nursing will decrease with age. In the meantime it may help you to know that more and more pediatricians recommend letting a baby nurse as much as she needs, as long as this works for you.

If you do start to find yourself getting fatigued from night nursing sessions, here are some tips to minimize them:

• Make sure your baby is eating well during the day. Sometimes babies of this age can be so busy experiencing life that they don't eat as much as they need, and then they're hungrier at night.

• If your baby doesn't eat much when there's a lot going on around her, make sure mealtime/nursing time is a calm and quiet affair.

• Instead of letting her nurse every time she wakes up at night, snuggle her, let her touch your breast, talk or sing to her softly, do whatever seems to help calm your baby and lull her back to sleep. That way, she won't come to expect the breast so much at night and may sleep for longer bouts. (If you want some detailed guidance on how to wean your baby from the breast at night, see "Ten Nights," page 170.)

Understand, though, that some babies who end up in the family bed are very strong willed, have greater needs, and will not easily give up the breast. For these babies, it's probably best to just let them taper off when they're ready or when you can reason with them a little better.

• If possible, let the baby's father take over some of the night-time comforting. When your baby awakens, dad might be able to soothe her back to sleep with cuddling, soft talking, and even explaining that everyone needs sleep, including mama's nippies/num-nums/whatever you're calling them. There are times when dancing with dad works. Other times, the baby's just got to nurse.

Q: Why does our baby always end up with his feet pushing against my husband's side, and his head in my armpit, or some similar strange positioning? This kid is taking up all the room on our bed! We're clinging to the edges for dear life half the time.

A: We find it amazing just how much room a little baby can take up. While some babies (and toddlers and young children) are content to remain parallel to their parents at night, others have a penchant for the perpendicular, creating what looks like a giant letter "H" in the family bed. This is probably because babies tend to be heat-seeking missiles, gravitating toward a cozy, warm parent when possible. It's a great survival tactic. And where the head goes, the feet usually follow at the opposite end. Voilà: a perfect letter "H." (Some theorize a baby moves to point north and south with his body. Others say it's east and west. We wouldn't bet the bank on either of these theories.) Babies seem perfectly happy with this setup, but it's not ideal for parents.

One way to take the "H" out of the "faHmily" bed is to get a bigger bed. A king-size bed will give you plenty of room to scoot out of your baby's way without scooting yourself off the bed. Another solution is to put your baby in a sidecar (see page 60 for more on this). If your child is a toddler, consider getting him a twin bed and pushing it up against yours (see page 154 for more details). Alternatively, you can move your baby to mom's side of the bed. If your baby is on one side of mom, but not next to dad, the number of people he can push into is cut in half. And often in this case, the baby just ends up snuggling closer to mom, not butting into her like a battering ram.

Q: Every time one of us rolls over or gets in or out of bed, the bed bounces a little and the baby wakes up. What can we do?

A: Consider investing in a futon. Futons—firm and spring-free—are great for quashing the ripple effect that can disturb whoever is sharing your bed. They're not too pricey, and you can either put yours directly on the floor (if allergies aren't a problem) or atop your existing box spring.

Q: I don't want to go to bed when my baby goes to bed (around 8:30 P.M.), but when she falls asleep and I try to sneak out of the bedroom to be with my husband or do some work, she inevitably wakes up before I've even tiptoed out the door. Tired as I am, and much as I like to sleep, I'm not usually ready to retire so early. Can you recommend anything to help me get away for a while?

Good Nights

A: Some family bed babies drop off and nothing can wake them. Others, like yours, need a little time before you can "sneak" away. The trick is to wait until your child is in a deep sleep before you make your move. Look for rhythmic breathing and lack of eye and limb movement (except for an occasional body jerk).

Exactly when this deeper sleep occurs depends on the age of your baby, according to Thomas M. Anders, M.D., professor of psychiatry at the University of California, Davis, School of Medicine, and director of the school's infant and family sleep laboratory.

For babies under six months, the wait for deeper sleep may take a while because young babies start sleep with a REM (rapid eye movement) period, in which they're more prone to waking. REM sleep is active sleep, and you'll see your baby's eyes moving under her lids, and her face or hands may twitch. Once that stops—it usually takes twenty to thirty minutes in a young baby—she'll be in an NREM (non-REM) period, and you should be able to make your move. It may seem like a long time to wait, but it's a small investment for a little free time.

For babies older than six months, Dr. Anders says the wait for the deeper NREM sleep is shorter. Generally speaking, within five to ten minutes, you should see the signs of deep sleep (some babies switch to this older baby pattern by just three months).

Of course, anytime you leave your baby sleeping alone, be sure she's safely in bed.

Keep in mind that the data on sleep stages are based on infants who don't routinely sleep in contact with a parent. (Almost all sleep research is done on solitary sleeping infants.

This is starting to change, but we have a long way to go.) While the timing of stages may be exactly the same for co-sleepers, we can't definitively say there won't be differences. If the timing doesn't match your child's sleep, see if you can determine her patterns yourself.

Q: Any ideas on how I can have a little time to myself while my baby naps? Right now she's at a point where she wakes up when I put her down for a nap, and I'm getting frustrated.

A: This question doesn't have the nice, neat sleep-stage answer the previous one did because naps are a different animal from nighttime sleep, and vary greatly. But there are a couple of tips we can give you:

If your baby takes two naps a day, your best bet for being able to leave her sleeping happily on her own is the afternoon nap. REM sleep (the active, lighter sleep stage) often predominates in morning naps, according to sleep expert Dr. Anders, and NREM sleep (deeper sleep, harder-to-wake baby) in afternoons. Wait until you see the signs of deep sleep mentioned in the previous answer, and then make your getaway after you're sure she's in a safe place. See "Naptime Notes," page 66, for more on safety for babies sleeping alone.

We also highly recommend "wearing" your baby in a sling or other kind of baby carrier during her naps. She'll likely sleep very well nestled beside your moving body, and you can get lots done while she sleeps. Granted, you won't be solo, and you won't be able to clean the oven or scrub the tub (darn!), but at least your hands and legs will be free.

Good Nights

Another possible solution for you is a baby swing. Some parents swear by baby swings, others swear at them, thinking of them as just another mechanical substitute for mom. In the same vein, some babies love swings, while others would swear at them if they could. We say if you need some time alone, and your baby is happy in the swing, let her take little naps in it.

Q: My toddler wakes up at 3:00 A.M. to start a conversation or play a game. At first it was cute and I had little chats with him, but it's been two weeks and I'm at my wit's end! What should I do?

A: If you want to put a stop to the night party, the only game you should play with him at that hour is possum: Just lie there and pretend to continue to sleep. When he sees no one is going to get up with him, he'll likely settle down and go back to sleep. Since you didn't do this right away it may take a few nights, but he'll soon get the idea that 3:00 A.M. is not party time. (If he's so insistent that it would be impossible for you to feign sleep, quietly tell him it's time for everyone to sleep, and that you're going to sleep and he needs to do the same. Then play possum again.)

A NOTE FROM DR. JAY: *I realize some parents don't mind getting up and chatting or playing. If you're a night person and want to get up and talk or play, go ahead. The consequences are there, but you'll survive, and your child will eventually start sleeping "normally" again.*

Q: How important is it to have a bedtime routine? I've never been a "schedule" person, but I'm thinking this might help my daughter sleep better.

A: Bedtime routines can help a baby figure out that there are certain times for certain activities, and that sleep is one of those "activities." They can also help a parent figure these things out.

If you think you or your baby would benefit from a schedule, by all means try it. Develop a routine that your little one comes to associate with sleep. Books, bath, nursing, brushing teeth, and snuggling together are part of many family bed parents' nighttime rituals. Add your own especially relaxing one, like a massage or a candle-lit bath (with candles safely out of the child's way, of course).

If you opt not to go all-out on bedtime routines, you'll be happy to know that in cultures where co-sleeping is the norm, bedtime routines are usually nonexistent.[1] In these cultures, and with many co-sleeping families in our culture, the reason this works may be because some of these children go to sleep at the same time as their parents, and it's a given that everyone just goes to sleep, no coercion needed. Or it may be that these children are allowed to fall asleep when they're naturally tired. As long as this doesn't interfere with daytime mood or plans, it's not usually a problem.

Q: Our three-year-old girl is a major night owl. No matter how we've tweaked her sleep schedule, she always stays up very late at night (early in the morning, to be more accurate!). Fortunately, my husband and I are night people too, and we enjoy her company, but she even outlasts us some nights. Friends look at us like we're horrible parents when we tell them her "schedule," but she always ends up getting enough sleep and is one of the happiest children I've seen. Should we be concerned?

A: You'll be relieved to know that the weight of responsibility for your daughter's atypical hours may be somewhat lifted off your shoulders by a recent scientific discovery: Some people have the propensity to be night owls (or, in the opposite case, morning larks) thanks to genetics.[2,3] "It seems that our parents—through their DNA—continue to influence our bedtimes," reports an article in the journal *Nature Medicine*.[4]

Since you and your husband are both night people, genetics could play a role in your daughter's late-night preference. But that doesn't mean her young years need to be filled with David Letterman and Conan O'Brien. While your child may never go to sleep when the sun sets, as many of her friends undoubtedly do, there are many ways you can help her move to an earlier schedule (if you so desire. Many families do well with a schedule like yours and see no need to alter it.)

- Make sure she gets enough exercise during the day. A child with a tired body is more likely to succumb to sleep than one who still hasn't gotten the energy out of her system. (Don't overdo it, of course. A stint at the playground or a fast-paced walk on the beach with the dog can do wonders.)

- If she seems to be giving up her afternoon nap, don't try to prolong it. While these naps are nice for you, even a short afternoon nap can provide night owl children with all the fuel it takes to jettison them wide awake into the wee hours. On the other hand, don't try to force her to stop napping if she still needs to sleep during the day. Contrary to popular belief, this isn't going to help your child sleep better at bedtime.

- Keep nighttime relatively dull, or at least calm. Children who like the night are often very active at night. Other children may bounce off the walls at night because they're overtired, but once they're in bed they usually fall asleep quickly. This isn't the case with night owls. They don't give a hoot that they're in bed, lights out—they're still raring to go. If you keep their environment peaceful—with books and soothing music instead of chasing games and videos, for instance—they'll be more inclined to recline earlier.

- Try to maintain bedtime rituals, as discussed in the previous tip. Your night owl might take a while to acclimate to any kind of routine. Nighttime rituals aren't the magic answer for these kids, but they do help.

- Shift her schedule gradually. If your child has been staying up until midnight, you can't expect her to be sleepy at 9:00 P.M. just because she's had a bath and a book. Adjust her bedtime slowly—anywhere from fifteen minutes to an hour every few days, whatever seems to work for you. As she sleeps earlier, she should start to wake up earlier, which in turn should help her feel tired earlier.

Sleeping Like a Baby

Is your baby sleeping through the night yet?"

You've likely been asked that question dozens of times if you have a little baby. Usually it's said in one breath, almost in one word: "Ishesleepingthroughthenightyet?" It's sort of the de rigueur question for new parents in our culture, almost a rite of passage into parenthood.

Some parents eagerly await the opportunity to boast about their baby's amazing talent for sleeping. Others loathe the question. "I feel like spitting up every time someone asks," says one mom.

The subject of sleeping through the night is one that obsesses many new parents. In industrialized cultures like ours, sleeping through the night is one of the big early goals we strive for with our babies—almost an obsession. It's become something of a litmus test for "good" parenting and "good" babies. When a baby fails to accommodate by a certain age, usually somewhere around four to six months, the baby is often seen as having a sleep problem, and pediatricians and other well-meaning folks give mountains of advice on how to eradicate the problem.

But in reality, babies who aren't sleeping through the night aren't aberrations. In fact it turns out that these babies actually have a much more normal and natural sleeping pattern than their longer-sleeping friends.*

What our society has come to view as the norm is actually based on very old data gathered on babies in the 1950s, the heyday of formula-fed, solitary sleeping babies. These babies tended to sleep long and hard—sometimes eight to ten hours straight at around four months.[5]

Those long sleep hours make even the people who study infant sleep-wake patterns scratch their heads: "Development of a long unbroken night sleep by the early age of four months is surprising when considered from an evolutionary viewpoint because human infants, like other primates, are physiologically adapted for frequent suckling and close physical contact with their mothers," write the authors of a study of infant sleep, published in *Pediatrics*,[6] the official journal of the American Academy of Pediatrics.

Despite the huge increase in the number of breast-fed babies since these baseline studies of 1950s formula-fed infants, today's babies are still being evaluated with the same measuring stick. This makes for a bad fit, since breast-fed infants wake more frequently than formula-fed babies. And when the breast-fed baby is in the family bed, there can be more night waking yet. (But as other studies and countless

---

* This isn't to say that all night waking is normal and nothing to be concerned about, although that's usually the case. It's important to discuss your child's awakenings with your pediatrician to rule out any possible physical causes. That way you can rest easier when they happen.

anecdotes have shown, rather than being an impediment to a good night's sleep, the family bed is where babies and parents tend to get the best sleep.)

With our current models of normal sleep based on this half-century-old, outdated data, is it any wonder that some 30 percent of children under age four are purported to have sleep problems? [7] (Big surprise: The greatest of these problems is the failure to sleep through the night.)

Some sleep researchers are calling for a revision of what constitutes normal sleep based on what today's babies eat and where they spend the night. Until this happens, next time your baby wakes in the middle of the night, realize that it's probably not your baby's problem; it's just that the definition of normal infant sleep needs a little updating.

Q: My toddler snores so loud he keeps us awake at night. We joked about it at first, calling him Mr. Buzzsaw, but now we're getting tired. Plus, he's getting grouchy during the day, and kind of hyper the way he does when he's really tired. What can we do?

A: Get thee to a pediatrician. Your child has the classic symptoms of sleep apnea, a disorder in which the upper airway becomes obstructed so he can't breathe properly while sleeping. (Snoring isn't always present in apnea, but some kind of breathing difficulty is usually detectable by parents.) The causes can be numerous, and include obesity and enlarged tonsils and adenoids. It could even be related to a dairy allergy. Your child's pediatrician should evaluate your child to determine what could be causing the apnea, and how (and if) it should be treated. The pediatrician may refer your son to an ear-nose-throat doctor, an allergist, or a sleep disorders clinic.

Be persistent in seeking care, because the problem is not always well recognized by pediatricians.

(Note: This type of apnea shouldn't be confused with new-born apnea, a life-threatening problem where the baby just stops breathing but not usually because of an obstruction.)

Q: What about burping my baby in bed? Do I attempt it or just let her sleep? The last thing I want to do is rouse her (and myself) out of a good sleep in order to burp her.

A: If your baby doesn't seem to have a gas problem, it's best to let sleeping babies lie. Why wake them up if they're sleeping happily?

If your baby seems uncomfortable after nursing and can't get back to sleep, do burp her. But most breast-feeding babies don't have to burp much. If you think your baby needs to burp for comfort, try it for a little bit (twenty to thirty seconds), but don't thump on her for ten minutes. If you have any questions or worries about your child's situation, ask your pediatrician. While your child's doctor may not approve of co-sleeping, the doctor should be willing and able to address your specific concerns.

Q: I'm afraid to let my eleven-month-old nurse at night anymore because she's got a few teeth, and I've heard night nursing is terrible for teeth. But she can't sleep without a little nursing before bed and maybe once at night. Am I giving her a mouthful of problems by letting her nurse at night?

Good Nights

A: The jury is still out on this one. Some pediatric dentists and pediatricians say night nursing doesn't have a bad effect on the teeth. When a baby or toddler has a cavity, they argue that it's more a function of the child's inherited enamel quality and daytime diet. Others say night nursing, while not as harmful to teeth as nighttime bottle-feeding, isn't doing a baby's teeth any favors.

Pediatric dentists do agree that breast-feeding is excellent for oral development and preventing malocclusion. Because of this, and all the other bountiful benefits of breast-feeding, we'd urge you not to wean your baby from the breast at night unless you're ready to wean her for other reasons.

If you choose to continue breast-feeding her at night, you should take her to a pediatric dentist to make sure her teeth are free of decay and that they don't have an enamel weakness that would pave the road to cavity city. (You may want to talk with other family bed parents to find a dentist who supports night nursing for children whose teeth are in good shape.) If the dentist thinks it's OK to continue night nursing, you'd be wise to not only brush your child's teeth before bedtime, but in the morning as well. That way you have a chance to get rid of plaque before it can do much harm.

Another benefit of consulting with a pediatric dentist is if your child doesn't like having her teeth brushed, the dentist can show you several ways to effectively clean her teeth. Your child is bound to enjoy—or at least not detest—one of these techniques.

Q: My husband is a light sleeper and is getting tired of waking up from the rustling and bumps and occasional noise of having our baby in bed. He often goes to work in a bad mood. How can he get more sleep?

A: If the baby is between you, the first thing to do is move him to your side of the bed only, or even into a sidecar. This way, your husband will be spared the bumping and thumping of Junior's body parts. That's all you may need to do.

If dad still wakes up every time you or the baby moves, it's probably because of the mattress conducting the bounces clean over to his side of the bed. As we mentioned earlier in the chapter, a futon can minimize this problem.

If it gets to the point where your husband is starting to sleep in another room on a regular basis because of the baby, you should have a heart-to-heart talk with him. You may have to weigh the benefits of co-sleeping with the possible detriment to your marriage. If this setup is something he doesn't mind, and you can maintain a close relationship during this (hopefully) short period, then you can probably feel more at ease about continuing co-sleeping. But if he harbors anger or resentment, you may have to re-evaluate the situation.

Q: Help! I'm tired of having to climb over to the other side of my baby to switch breasts when nursing in bed. It's also very disturbing to her when I lift her up to go to my other side to nurse after she's done on one side. We're both very awake after these maneuvers. Any suggestions?

A: Your night nursing life is about to be made much easier. Instead of the nighttime acrobatics you've been doing, when you're done nursing on the "bottom" breast, just lean farther over your baby so your "top" breast hangs low enough for her to latch onto. (You don't have to be Dolly Parton for this move.) See illustration on next page.

Some moms find their back gets stiff in this leaning posi-

tion. If this happens to you, a pillow or bolster behind your
back or under your "top" knee can work wonders.

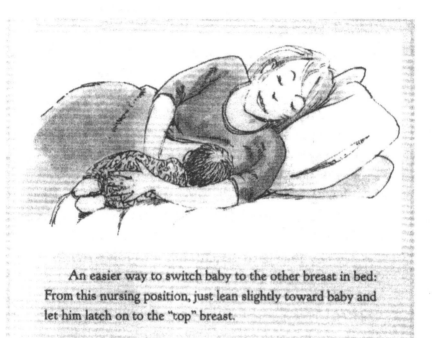

An easier way to switch baby to the other breast in bed:
From this nursing position, just lean slightly toward baby and
let him latch on to the "top" breast.

Q: In three months we're expecting our second child, and
our two-year-old son is still in bed with us. I don't think he's
ready to move into his own bed yet, and I really don't mind if
he stays. But I don't know how we can make it work with two
kids and two parents. What should we do?

A: Your son may not care to move out of bed *yet*, but his
own bed may start looking mighty appealing to him when the
new baby takes up residency in your bed. In fact, a top reason

children leave the family bed is because of the arrival of a new sibling there. As Angie, a mother of a three year old and a newborn, told us, "Our son put up with the decreased space, the baby noises, and my waking for night feedings for two nights. On the third night, he asked if he could sleep in his own bed, and that was that."

If you think your son will opt to stay on, you may want to consider creating more space by having him move to his own twin bed pushed right up flush beside yours. If you can get it at the same level, it's more like an extension of your own bed, and he may well enjoy the extra space of his "big boy" bed. The big benefit is safety, since you don't want to be like a tin of sardines when the baby arrives.

Another option for your bed setup is to place mattresses or futons on the floor, side by side. (As we mentioned earlier, if you're going to do this, make sure the floors are as free of dust as possible so allergies don't become an issue.) A few families we've interviewed have had a room filled with wall-to-wall mattresses for them and their two or three (or in one case, four) children. These parents have warm and fuzzy memories of waking up in the morning with little limbs and faces everywhere. "I wouldn't trade those times for anything in the world," says one such den mother.

Whatever setup you choose, it's important that your infant doesn't sleep beside your older child. Sleeping children don't always have the same awareness of their surroundings as adults and can pose a hazard to a baby.

A final note: We advise any parent who will be changing the bed setup because of a new baby to make any changes at least a few months before the baby's arrival. That way the child doesn't see the baby as displacing him.

Birds Do It, Beasts Do It

I f you're still wondering if sleeping next to your baby is copacetic, it may help you to look to nature: Just about any animal that cares for its young—most birds and mammals—sleeps with its young.

"There is virtually no exception where an animal takes care of its young but leaves them alone to sleep," says animal behaviorist Lucie Salwiczek, Ph.D., of the Max-Planck-Institute for Behavioral Physiology in Germany. (Although some birds and mammals do hunt or forage for food at times while their young sleep.)

We may not want to draw too many comparisons to our more distant animal relatives because they often have parenting habits that humans wouldn't want to share. Mice moms, for instance, do sleep with their baby mice, but they're also prone to eating them.

So we look to our closest animal relatives—nonhuman primates. And indeed no infant monkeys or apes sleep alone. According to James Anderson, Ph.D., who specializes in nonhuman primate behavior at the University of Stirling, Scotland, infant Old World monkeys and apes sleep snuggled together with their mothers. In some cases there may be a huddle of animals sleeping together, so that the infant might be sandwiched between the mother and another monkey. This goes on until weaning, and even beyond.

The great apes (chimpanzees, gorillas, orangutans, and bonobos) sleep in nests they make at dusk, with infants sleeping with their mothers for four or five years, when a new infant is born, says Anderson. This occasionally goes on longer, especially if the mother has no new surviving offspring.

Since 98 to 99 percent of our DNA is identical to that of chimpanzees (less so with other great apes), it shouldn't come as a shock that we might have an inclination to sleep beside our young as well. The pull of our genes isn't dismissed just because we may have an adorable nursery down the hall and an armload of books on getting a baby to sleep in a crib.

And in case you were looking for some examples of animals who don't sleep with their young:

Cockroaches don't co-sleep. Neither do snakes, crabs, tarantulas, or fleas.

(We admit these are unappealing examples, but they're great to casually mention in passing when talking with a particularly venomous family bed skeptic.)

Q: Everyone around us is telling us we have to train our baby to sleep by letting him cry it out, but I just don't have the heart to do this. We actually tried it for a night, and he never stopped crying and I couldn't stand it. One of the books says: "Believe it or not, leaving your child alone to cry in bed is a way to show your love and care for him." (*Baby & Toddler Sleep Program*, by John Pearce, M.D.) What do you think?

A: Ah, you've picked a subject we feel so strongly about that we're going to devote the remainder of the chapter to it.

For readers unfamiliar with crying it out, we'll start with a description of what crying it out involves.

It's a grueling scene that's repeated thousands of times a night, every night, all over the country. Tired parents clutch a book that promises to train their baby to sleep better. But their baby is not sleeping. He is crying. His cries are piercing and panicked. The parents pace. They've followed the book's instructions exactly, and they can't give up now. They turn up the TV to drown out their baby. But even though he's in his crib down the hall, behind the closed door of the nursery, his frantic cries still cut through.

By now one or both parents may be struggling to overcome the instinct deep in their gut to rush to the baby's room, pick him up, comfort him, and abandon the whole project. But they persist. After all, their pediatrician says it's the thing to do, and their friends do, and the book certainly does. What does instinct have to do with it?

In the end, the baby often does begin to sleep through the night via these cry-it-out techniques. It could take minutes or hours over several days or weeks—sometimes even months. This is how millions of Americans have learned to sleep.

At least eight popular sleep-training books advocate letting an infant cry it out in order for him to understand that bedtime is time for sleep—more to the point, for sleeping alone—not for snuggles and comfort and love. The idea behind these techniques is that if you don't respond to the crying, you don't reinforce it, and the crying stops and the baby sleeps.

Each of these books espouses a different method for how to go about letting a baby cry. Some have complicated formulas for the varying lengths of time parents need to wait to check on their child. At least two advocate letting a child cry for as long as it takes for him to fall asleep. The books often claim they'll help you learn to respect your baby's needs and rhythms, but then they turn right around and teach you how to disrespect and ignore your little baby as he does his best to communicate his needs for closeness and food.

(Note: We don't like cry-it-out techniques, but in fairness, they can be helpful to parents at their wit's end who aren't willing to try the family bed, or who have one too many kids awake at night. We'd rather see sleep training done in a controlled setting than parents who are so overtired that they're angry and potentially out of control with their children. On page 170, we describe a kinder, toned-down sleep-training method for older babies whose parents are desperate to have them sleep long chunks. Our hearts are not in this technique, since it can involve crying, but it's more humane than the popular sleep-training methods that some parents would otherwise resort to.)

Just What the Doctor Didn't Order

With all the cry-it-out advice out there, it's rare to hear the voices of experts who think it's less than ideal. But a growing number of physicians and psychologists are beginning to speak out against this practice. Here's what a few have to say:

Mizin Kawasaki, M.D., Los Angeles pediatrician: "It's inhumane. If an adult would be crying like that, so helpless and frightened, it would be cruel and abusive to ignore them. It's even more unconscionable to make babies cry all alone like this, but our society sees it as OK because it's 'just' a baby."

David Servan-Schreiber, M.D., Ph.D., neuroscientist and clinical associate professor of psychiatry at the University of Pittsburgh School of Medicine: "Maternal separation is a universal cross-species potent stressor. It's the babies with sensitive temperaments who are most affected by crying it out. What do they learn? They learn that their need for warmth and reassurance is a character flaw; that parents are cold, distant figures; that fear and loneliness are the expected currency of existence. They learn that important figures in one's emotional world cannot be trusted to understand and respond with a caring attitude.

"Since their need is inborn and cannot be controlled, they often adjust by either withdrawing and removing themselves from their emotions (depressive tendencies as adults) or by learning how to manipulate and control others who won't give

96

freely when it is so needed (oppositional, antisocial tendencies) or by learning later to soothe loneliness and pain not with people, but with means that, to them, seem more reliable, such as alcohol or drugs."

Michael L. Commons, Ph.D., Harvard University lecturer on psychiatry: "Cortisol (a hormone secreted during stressful situations, such as crying it out) . . . makes you more prone to the bad effects of future stress, it makes you more prone to mental illness and it makes it harder to recover from stress."[8]

William Sears, M.D., pediatrician and author of several parenting books: "A baby's cries are a baby's language. Primitive though it may be, crying is a tiny baby's only network of communication to the outside world. Taking away this form of communication may have a carry-over effect on the general desire to communicate to caregivers. . . . As the baby loses trust in his ability to communicate, he also loses trust that the caregiver will respond. The 'let cry' advice may produce a short-term gain, but a long-term loss."[9]

Sleep Training
Ad Nauseam

Several popular sleep-training books discuss a problem that befalls many babies while "learning" to sleep via the cry-it-out methods they espouse: Babies can cry so hard while alone in their cribs that they throw up.

One would think that at this point the gig would be up, and the books' authors would show some empathy, advising parents to go in, comfort their babies, and forget about sleep training, at least for the night. But alas, one would be wrong.

Here's what a few of these sleep-training books say about babies vomiting under duress, and how they recommend handling the situation:

• "Vomiting is no big deal for infants and toddlers, although it can be quite upsetting for parents. For young children, vomiting can even be fun. And it is common for infants and toddlers to vomit after crying for a long period of time. Unfortunately children can also learn to vomit at will if vomiting is reinforced. It gets parents to respond. And it gets the child out of the crib. . . . If your baby vomits after crying, don't worry about it and don't reinforce it. Be neutral. Change the sheets, clean up the baby as well as you can (preferably without picking him up), and leave the room."

—*SLEEPING THROUGH THE NIGHT*,

BY JODI A. MINDELL, PH.D.[10]

• "Vomiting does not hurt your child, and you do not have to feel guilty."

—*SOLVE YOUR CHILD'S SLEEP PROBLEMS*,

RICHARD FERBER, M.D. (DR. FERBER

ALSO ADVOCATES "DISTANT" CLEANUP

PROCEDURES SIMILAR TO MINDELL'S.[11])

• "Your child literally may scream himself sick. Don't fuss over him when he's sick, even if it has ruined the carpet. Go in with two towels. Use one to wipe up the vomit and the other to put over the damp spot. Don't talk to your child. . . . And don't look your child in the face. Say your usual goodnight phrase and leave the room."

—*BABY & TODDLER SLEEP PROGRAM*,

JOHN PEARCE, M.D.[12]

• "If the vomiting is irregular and occasional, you should try waiting until after you think she is deeply asleep before checking, and then quickly clean her if needed."

—FROM A CHAPTER ON SLEEP TRAINING FOR

BABIES AS YOUNG AS FOUR MONTHS OLD,

FROM THE BOOK *HEALTHY SLEEP HABITS,*

HAPPY CHILD, MARC WEISSBLUTH, M.D.[13]

(We didn't realize that falling asleep in one's own vomit was a healthy sleep habit.)

It's perhaps not a coincidence that all four of these books contain sections on head banging. Dr. Ferber's book contains a vivid description of what head banging looks like:

"If your child bangs his head he probably gets up on all fours and rocks back and forth, hitting his forehead or the top of his head into the headboard of the crib or bed. Or he may sit in bed and bang backwards into the headboard. Some children will lie face down and lift their heads, or head and chest, then bang or drop back into the pillow or mattress again and again. Occasionally a child may stand in his crib, hold on to the side rail, and hit his head there. Now and then a child will assume a very awkward posture to allow himself to rock, bang his head, suck his thumb, and hold on to a stuffed animal at the same time."[14]

This is so sad, and one would think so abnormal. But Mindell reassures us: "Babies often rock or bang their heads to fall asleep. This is normal."[15]

Dr. Weissbluth strolls down memory lane and talks about how his third son banged his head against the crib every night after they moved to a new house. "My solution was to use clothesline rope and sofa cushions to pad both ends and both sides completely. Now, when he banged away, there was no racket, no pain, and no parental attention." His son stopped within a few days, but he says "other parents are not so lucky," with 5 to 10 percent of children banging or rolling their heads before falling asleep for the first few years.[16]

We have news for these sleep experts: Head banging is not normal. Family bed children don't do it.

Perhaps if bedtime were a more gentle, loving time—a time without fear and crying and vomiting—these babies would take up another hobby. (Nursing, cooing, and cuddling are a few that come to mind.)

Just the Facts, Mom

As more scientists examine the effects of cry-it-out sleep training, it's becoming evident that some of the assumptions at the core of these techniques are just plain incorrect. Here are a few myths in particular we feel it's imperative to address:

Myth: It can't hurt them.

Fact: Putting your baby through cry-it-out sleep training isn't the worst thing you can do to him, but it's far from the best. We know of no studies on short-term effects or even possible subtle, long-term effects of crying it out in humans. But studies of parent-infant separation involving "crying" in nonhuman primates show that the hormonal stress response of babies in these situations can be "equivalent to or greater than that induced by physical trauma."[17]

In addition, similar studies have found that stressful sepa-

ration situations can have an adverse effect on immune function.[18] While most children are very resilient and probably
won't experience long-term problems from crying it out,
we can't be certain of its effects on more sensitive children.
(The pro's on pages 96–97 do describe some serious potential
consequences.)

Myth: It's good for their lungs.

Fact: Babies do not by any means need to scream and cry
alone in a crib in order to exercise their lungs. The simple act
of breathing is all the exercise their lungs need. (If crying is
good for the lungs, next thing you know some doctor will try
to convince you that bleeding is good for the heart. Wait. They
tried to do that a long time ago.)

Myth: It always works.

Fact: Some babies just don't respond the way cry-it-out
pundits expect. Even famed child sleep expert Richard Ferber,
M.D., admits that some children are not trainable.[19] They just
keep crying.

Even when it works initially, babies and young children
often go through periods in their development where they
need a "refresher" course. Sometimes these are effective, sometimes not. Often, sleep training is even more grueling for parents and children the second and third time around.

Myth: Your child will be spoiled if you always respond to
his cries.

Fact: You can't spoil a baby. Showing a little baby that you love him enough to respond to his crying day and night only serves to bolster your bond and makes the baby feel as if he's worthy of being heard. (It's not at all the same as giving a persistent three year old a piece of cake he's been whining for before dinner. Older kids can indeed be spoiled.)

Unfortunately, many Americans feel strongly that little babies are imminently spoilable: A recent survey found that 62 percent of adults believe a six-month-old baby can be spoiled. The survey also found that 44 percent of parents of young children and 60 percent of grandparents believe picking up a three month old every time he cries will spoil the child.[20] The experts don't concur.

"If you don't pick up a baby when he is crying, you can build up his levels of stress and distress," says Kyle Pruett, M.D., clinical professor of psychiatry at the Yale Child Study Center. "Responding to your child's needs is not spoiling. Young children need your attention to develop the faith and trust that their needs matter to you."[21]

Of even greater importance to pooped parents, studies show that maternal responsiveness to crying in young babies leads to babies who actually cry less when they're older. Conversely, babies whose mothers often ignore their cries early on tend to cry more frequently. As one study notes: "The more unresponsive the mother, the more the baby cries, and his crying seems to make her more reluctant than ever to respond."[22]

Myth: The baby stopped crying; he couldn't be upset.

Good Nights

Fact: In studies of infant monkeys separated from their mothers, vocalizations (crying) generally declined dramatically across six separations. On the surface, it looked as though the infants had become used to their mothers not responding and weren't troubled by it.

But these babies weren't as content as they appeared. When researchers checked their blood levels of the stress hormone cortisol, it remained consistently high. Even when checked after eighty separations, the hormonal stress response was still elevated. So even though the babies were quiet, they were still feeling the ill effects of separation.[23]

There's been no equivalent study of human infants, so we can't be sure our babies react the same way. But anecdotal evidence shows that some babies become extremely clingy after a cry-it-out night. It's one of the few ways they can show their dismay about events of the past night.

"She screamed for hours," recounts Erin, whose daughter was six months when someone convinced Erin to train her to sleep. "After that she needed me to be in her sight all day. If I went around a corner, she went nuts, screaming and crying. After a few more days, she was literally sitting on my feet if I was not holding her.... I even had to take her to the bathroom with me." Eventually Erin gave up and brought her daughter into her bed. She says the family bed helped both her and her daughter get over the trauma of sleep training, "but it took a while."

5.

Love in the Laundry Room

Keeping the Sizzle in Your Sex Life

The first question people ask family bedders is usually something along these lines: "But what about—you know—sex?"

It's easy to understand the curiosity, although it's awfully nosy of people to ask. (More on this later.) Just being a parent can make it difficult to find the time and energy to make love, and a drooling little bundle between you and your partner doesn't do much to fan the flames of ardor. It can be all too easy to mumble to your interested mate, "Not tonight, dear, I have a baby foot on my shoulder."

Certainly, the popular "train your baby to sleep" press does a good job of perpetuating this image. Countless articles and books would have you believe that by letting your baby sleep in your bed, you'll have the sex life of a cloistered nun until your child leaves for college. A typical statement about co-sleeping, which leaves little room for doubting such a demise: ". . . it is deadly to your sex life," writes Jodi Mindell, in her book, *Sleeping Through the Night.*[1]

But the truth is most family bed parents actually have very satisfying sex lives. Many, like Bob, a family bed dad and business insurance underwriter, say sex is even better than before the baby came along.

"I thought the family bed would kind of mess up our love life," says Bob. "But actually, hard as it is to believe, it's helped improve it."*

While we've talked with our share of parents (family bed and not) who are too pooped to party, the majority of family bed parents who took part in our research said sex was better than or as good as it was before the family bed. There are a couple of explanations for this:

- *More love between parents:* The sense of unity family bed couples can feel knowing they're raising their children in a tender, compassionate way makes them feel closer to each other. This can beget more loving and tenderness between the parents. As one mom put it, "We've chosen to unite as a family, which in turn makes my husband and me feel more secure and loving in our own relationship. . . . Our sex life is better for it." Parents who don't practice co-sleeping might feel the same way, but we've heard this explanation time and time again from family bedders.

- *More creativity:* Family bed parents find it nearly impossible to just roll over, make love, and fall back to sleep. There's

---

* We granted name anonymity to parents regarding their sex lives. With the exception of the first parent we quoted in this chapter, parents' names will not be used here.

this cute little critter in bed that gets in the way of this, in more ways than one. So most family bedders simply choose to take sex out of the bedroom. The results: Sizzling, adventurous, put-the-spark-back-in-the-marriage sex.

In addition, parents whose babies had a rough time learning to sleep in their bassinet or crib are happy to discover what the family bed can do for their libidos. "I find sex better when I have enough sleep," says a Maryland mom of two young children. "The family bed lets me get much, much more sleep."

It's not foolproof, of course. Some parents complain that the family bed has stood in the way of a good sex life. But there are many ways around the inconveniences caused by the family bed, if both parents are willing to work a little harder.

Between the Sheets . . . Not!

Family bed parents aren't likely to lead boring sex lives. The expression, "between the sheets," doesn't have much meaning for them unless a rendezvous happens to take them to their guest room. For obvious reasons, most parents choose not to make love in the same bed where their child is sleeping. "I can't even 'do it' in front of the cat," says a co-sleeping mom.

So family bed parents have to be more creative. Take sex out of the bedroom, and the rest of the house—and beyond—becomes fair game. "It opens up all kinds of possibilities," says syndicated sex advice columnist Isadora Alman. "Adding a new bit of pizzazz, like a change of place or time, can really heat things up."

Good Nights

As long as your child is safely on the family bed (see chapter 3), and you can hear him if he needs you, or if he's being watched by a sitter or friend or relative while you go out, the world is your oyster, so to speak. For many parents it's the best thing that's happened to their sex lives.

- "It got us out of the rut we were in."

    —A MOTHER OF THREE

- "I have not made love in bed for nearly two years now, and I can honestly say that I don't miss it and that our sex life is wonderful, varied, frequent, and satisfying."

    —A MOTHER OF A TODDLER

- "We feel like teenagers again!"

    —A MOTHER OF A YOUNG BABY

- "I'm creative anyway. This just enhanced the creativity."

    —A FATHER OF THREE

Location, Location, Location

Because we're so entrenched in the idea that the bed is the place to make love (witness phrases like "She slept with him," or "He took her to bed"), figuring out alternative locations doesn't necessarily come easily. Parents new to the family bed can be stymied, especially if their lovemaking before the baby didn't include a variety of locations.

Here's something that should make it a little easier. Most family bed parents follow this simple tenet when it comes to location selection: Make love anywhere the baby is not.

As one dad put it, "Anywhere but a cold floor will do, although we may have even done that before." Not specific enough? Should you need a little help to get your imagination moving in the right direction, check out our list of the Top Ten Places Family Bed Parents Make Love.

Top Ten Places Family Bed Parents Make Love

(based on the 250 family bed parents who took part in our research)

1. Living room couch
2. Living room floor
3. Shower
4. Guest room (in the bed)
5. Back or front yard
6. Car, while on a date (The number of family bed parents who go "parking" is remarkable.)
7. Kitchen counter or table
8. Baby's empty nursery/child's empty bedroom

9. Bathroom floor or counter
10. The great outdoors (Camping seems to be a popular pastime among co-sleepers.)

Of course, the locales don't stop there. Some other favorite spots mentioned by parents: In the pool, on a pool table, in the playpen, in a lake, on the porch, on the floor of a walk-in closet, in a hammock, at the office, in the bathroom of a restaurant, on a trampoline, in the hot tub, on the clothes dryer, on the clothes washer, in a pay-by-the-hour motel, in the basement, and, of course, on that old standby, the dining room table.

If the challenge of finding a place to make love still seems a bit daunting, it might help you to hear some words of wisdom from parents of teenagers (no longer in the family bed, of course): "You've got it easy when your child is little," says a mom of two grown children. "With a newborn/toddler, they stay where you put them and you have the whole house to yourselves.... Later the teenager has the whole house and you only have your bedroom available." Her advice: Go find yourself a nice little nook for some nooky while there's still time.

Making Time for Making Love

None of the preceding tips will do you much good, however, if you can't find the time or energy for sex. Parenthood alone, exhausting as it is, can be enough to zap the libido right out of you. Whether you're a family bedder or not, after parenthood you usually have to work a little harder to make your sex life have that pre-parenthood spark again.

The good news is that family bed parents generally share the same strategy as other parents: They wait until the children are asleep. It's simple. And it works, especially if you have a child who sleeps for long stretches. (Be sure your little one is sleeping in a safe place, of course, and not, for instance, rolling slowly toward the edge of the bed while you're out of the room. For information on safe napping/solitary sleep setups, see "Naptime Notes," page 66.)

A little planning can make your time together even more special. Make a date, and revel in the waiting. Even the Queen Mother of sex advice, Dr. Ruth Westheimer, gives planning two thumbs-up:

"... just because your life together—and sex—can't be spontaneous doesn't mean it can't be fun. In fact, by making dates to be with each other, you can prepare for your special evenings and make them seem memorable," Dr. Ruth writes. "The key word is anticipation. If you know that tonight's the night, you can allow yourself to fantasize in advance—and plan to make some of your fantasy come true. For new parents, such planned time together usually turns out much better than attempting to have sex on a catch-as-catch-can basis."[2]

Good Nights

Some parents worry that preparing for intimate encounters might make them seem too contrived, too planned. But parents who plan ahead say it's actually been great for their sex lives.

"I think communicating our needs and then waiting in anticipation has really strengthened our marriage and improved our love life tremendously!" says a mother of two.

Of course, just as the bed isn't the only place to make love, bedtime isn't the only time to make love. In fact many family bed parents find it easier to work daytime encounters into their schedules.

"Afternoons are much, much niftier," says a family bed dad about the time of day he and his wife prefer to make love.

Planning is still a necessary component for many family bedders, day or night. But during the day, there's often more chance for spontaneity. After all, babies and toddlers nap. Young children might watch a video or play with siblings or be in preschool.

These "early encounters," planned or not, are the mainstay for many family bed parents:

- "A Teletubbies tape and the Exersaucer have become a friend to us. I think we both get frisky when we hear Teletubbies theme music!"

  —A MOTHER OF A TODDLER

- "Our favorite date is having our kids go to a friend's house for a couple of hours and we rent a movie and get take-out food to enjoy during the movie. Then we make love in a kid-free house before having the kids come home. We like doing the movie/take-out combo because a separate dinner and movie would take us away from our baby too long."

—A MOTHER OF TWO

- "My husband has a long lunch break, which is nice."

—A MOTHER OF FOUR FORMER FAMILY BEDDERS

- "We sometimes wait until our daughter is interested in a computer program."

—A MOTHER OF A PRESCHOOLER

- "When [our son] is taking a nap, we sneak into the guest room to make love...I think it makes the whole thing more exciting."

—A MOM OF A TODDLER

- "We have time together in the morning shower....It's definitely more spontaneous. If there's a moment, we take it."

—A MOTHER OF THREE

- "We once made love on the bathroom rug in my mother-in-law's house when we were on a trip there and she was playing with the baby. (She thought we were showering and getting ready—we think!)"

—A NEW MOM

"Sexdar"

Did you ever notice that just as you and your partner are getting into the heat of the moment, there's a little whimper that doesn't come from either of you? Then that whimper turns into a little cry, and if you don't tend to it quickly, the little cry becomes a loud wail.

This frustrating phenomenon, more efficient than a bucket of cold water at cooling the passion (at least temporarily), is common enough that we've given it a name: "Sexdar." It seems that young breast-fed babies, particularly those who co-sleep, have a built-in sense of bad timing for awakening. There are various theories about this "sexdar." A popular one holds that an infant smells the milk that may drip from the mother's breasts during her arousal. (Why this olfactory omniscience happens when parents are a few rooms away is baffling though.) Another attributes the baby's awakening to a mysterious psychic connection with the mother that may help prevent pregnancy too early.

We know one couple who thought their baby had strong "sexdar" until they realized what she actually had was very sensitive hearing combined with parents who were a bit on the vocal side when they made love (in another room). "When we got quieter, she stayed asleep," says the dad.

Whatever the cause of "sexdar," there's not much you can do about it except persevere (and perhaps check the volume on your lovemaking). Like so many things in your child's life, this too shall pass.

Deeper Than Sex

All this said, the most important aspect of a happy, long-term sexual relationship isn't your technique, or your location, or how often you do it. You can incorporate all the sex tips in the world into your life together, but they won't get you far if the desire for your mate isn't there—and not just sexual desire, a desire to simply be together, to be friends, to be able to open up and talk, to "be there" for each other. Many sex therapists believe that if you have respect and love for each other, and an intimacy beyond sex, the sex itself will often follow naturally.

Parents in general, and family bed parents in particular, need to make sure they're able to have this nonsexual level of intimacy. You don't have to "take a break" from your children in order to achieve this. Intimacy can grow around the children, through the family. But it often helps to have a little time alone together to be with each other in a nonsexual way. Many parents make a point of having a "date night" once every week or two. Others snuggle and read or talk or watch a video when the kids go to sleep.

Singer-songwriter Kenny Loggins, whose children have

all slept in the family bed, knows about maintaining parental intimacy.

"Like most parents, we have to make that [time alone] happen. . . . Mom's pretty exhausted at night, so we make what we call Date Day. Once a week we have this time to be together, whether we make love or not, or whether we just walk on the beach, we always try to find the time to talk to each other in a deep, honest way," Loggins told a reporter on *Home & Garden Television* during a tour of his California home (which included a visit to his sumptuous master bedroom, complete with gigantic family bed).[3]

Sometimes it's a simple, loving, nonsexual act that's the catalyst to good sex. One dad says his wife "gets cozier" with him because of how amenable he is to the family bed and family closeness. One mom says she felt such overwhelming love for her husband one day after seeing how carefully and kindly he dressed and fed their baby that "I just melted for him" when the baby went to sleep.

"Would any man ever assume that the way to his wife's bed is through diapering their baby?" asks sex advice columnist Alman. "This is better than flowers and candy for many parents. It's genuine."

Acts of tenderness and caring by the father may, in fact, be more appreciated by the mother in the months after the baby is born than at any other time of life. Certainly, any help from the father can alleviate some of the mother's exhaustion, but the reason for this heightened responsiveness to loving acts goes even deeper:

The hormone oxytocin, which is in abundant supply in moms postpartum, and especially during breast-feeding,[4] is known as "the hormone of love." Moms holding and nursing their newborns often feel a state of unparalleled euphoria. This same hormone, in its surprising "night shift" job, also happens to reach high levels during lovemaking.[5] "Perhaps this is why love, tenderness, and sexual pleasure are so intimately related in a woman's experience," says David Servan-Schreiber, M.D., Ph.D., neuroscientist and clinical associate professor of psychiatry at the University of Pittsburgh Medical School.

"This makes the mother exquisitely sensitive to tender and kind gestures from her partner and, more than anything else, to demonstrations of caring toward her baby," says Dr. Servan-Schreiber. "The father who openly shares his love for his baby and supports the mother's need for closeness and connectedness may find that the mother's sensual enthusiasm can reach heights he never suspected."

Of course the early postpartum weeks (and often months) are usually a big time-out period for sex. Some cultures even have taboos against sex during the first couple of years postpartum.[6]

But even after you can physically make love again, sometimes the desire just isn't there. Nursing moms may feel completely "touched out" and not want another mouth or pair of hands all over them. Even very involved new dads may feel something akin to this. It's more common, though, for new dads to feel they've been replaced. If they feel left out, they can become withdrawn.

At times like these, the baby is sometimes used as a kind of shield against sex. If this continues for a prolonged period, it can harm a relationship—sometimes irreversibly. The father who told us the following story is now going through a divorce:

"Nursing and sleeping with our son apparently satisfied

every physical need that my wife had. . . . She was never a cuddly person, but there was very little, progressing to almost no,
physical affection (let alone sex) between us for two years. . . .
[Her] physical contact with [our son] seems to have completely
obviated any need for contact with me, and I think this created
emotional distance also. . . . It turns out that even worse than to
be painfully lonely and alone in bed is when you are not alone
but instead are a body length away from a partner who is 100
percent certain to reject any advances, even just a request for
cuddling."

(This dad, remarkably, says the family bed is not to blame
for the demise of his marriage. He maintains that intimacy
problems went beyond the family bed and were there before
having children.)

Therapists recommend that parents realize they each have
special needs after the birth of a child. If one parent is "touched
out," the other should recognize this and try for nonphysical
intimacy. This can be anything from a fun date together to a
good talk to just relaxing and watching TV together. If the
"touched out" parent doesn't mind just a little touching, a massage, a tender kiss on the neck, or simply holding hands can
work wonders for closeness. The parent who isn't "touched
out" can also try to take over some of the child care to give the
more tired parent a break.

For the parent who is not as interested in sex, experts
advise that if there's any feeling of affection or empathy for the
partner who is interested in sex, to try to accommodate at least
a little—even if that only means asking for some more time. Dr.
Jay tells parents they have obligations beyond being mom and
dad—that they owe it to their kids to be husband and wife,

partner and partner, to create the most secure and happy relationship possible so the family can thrive.

"Don't just ignore the other person," says Lysa Parker, cofounder of Attachment Parenting International, a worldwide organization providing information and support to parents. "It's very important not to let the sexual relationship go down the drain. It's not good for the parents, but it's also bad for the children. One parent can come to resent the children being in bed, and that's the last thing you want."

A Last Retort

As anyone who shares a bed with a baby or young child knows, people are oh so curious about not only *if* you manage to have sex but *how* you manage to have sex, and they don't usually hesitate to ask. Somehow, sleeping with your baby seems to give strangers carte blanche to inquire about details of your sex life. If you're a co-sleeper and you haven't heard questions like, "Do you ever have sex?" "Doesn't that ruin your sex life?" "Where do you have sex?" "How often do you have sex?" and "Isn't your poor husband suffering?" consider yourself in the lucky minority.

Sometimes the person asking the question is genuinely interested because he or she might be considering co-sleeping or might have a close friend or relative thinking about it. More often, the person asking is curious for curiosity's sake (read: *nosy*). Perhaps there's even a touch of condescension or smugness in the interrogator's tone.

Depending on how the question strikes you, you can

ignore it, you can explain how your love life works, or you can come back with a quick retort, like these tried-and-true remarks other parents have brandished:

- "I ask why they're concerned about our sex life."

  —A MOTHER OF A TODDLER

- "I'll say, 'We make love frequently. How 'bout you?'"

  —A MOTHER OF THREE CHILDREN,
  AGES THIRTEEN YEARS TO
  SEVEN MONTHS

- "We just smile and tell them not to worry about us."

  —A MOM OF A YOUNG TODDLER

- "I say, 'We had four kids in six years. Anything else you'd care to know?'"

  —A DAD WHOSE FOUR KIDS ARE EIGHT
  TO TWO YEARS OLD

- "I usually ask them when was the last time I asked them about their sex life. That normally stops the questions."

  —A MOM OF TWO

- "Considering I've been pregnant five times since [our first daughter] moved into our bed, I just laugh."

  —A MOTHER OF FOUR

- "I just say 'It's called creativity,' and I give 'em a knowing wink."

  —A FATHER OF THREE

6.

Critical Support
Coping with Naysayers

Z Z Z Z Z Z Z Z Z Z Z Z Z Z Z Z Z

Your pediatrician shakes her head and gives you her best cry-it-out pep talk. Your best friend asks if your baby is *still* in your bed. Your father-in-law warns you that "that baby" will never learn to be independent. And your grandmother tells you she thinks you're just plain crazy to allow your child in your bed.

Everyone seems to have an opinion of the family bed, and it's not always a glowing one. Some critics have genuine concerns about the well-being of your baby, of your marriage, or both. Others just have a knee-jerk reaction against sharing a bed with anyone but an adult (or in many cases, a dog or cat!). "No way I'd do that with *my* kids," is one of the more common comments we hear from the less enthralled.

Whatever the motive, and whoever the critic, negative words about the family bed can sting. In some cases criticism can even make otherwise happy family bed parents move their baby to the previously unoccupied crib.

It's easy to say "just ignore the critics," and for some parents, it's easy to do. Dads, it seems, can be particularly adept at this. "I generally ignore their comments," says family bed dad Tom, whose wife meanwhile was losing sleep over criticism about their family bed. Or, as Kevin, father of a one-year-old family bed boy, maintains: "Tell the critics to kiss your $%#."

It's also easy to advise "just listen to your instincts." Again, for some parents, this is a cinch. These parents gleefully go with their gut, thumbing their noses at naysayers. But instincts may not be as strong for other parents. And even if they're strong, instincts can tangle with in-laws, other more experienced parents, health care workers, magazine articles, child-rearing books, and even total strangers. The result: Big doubts about where the little one sleeps.

So You Think *You* Have It Bad (Critics Hall of Fame)

Sometimes it can make you feel better about your own situation to see someone else who's got it worse. (Like the Arab proverb about the man who was feeling sorry for himself because he had no shoes until he met a man who had no feet.)

With this in mind, we bring you a few quick tales of some rotten remarks, audacious actions, and copious criticisms leveled at other family bed parents. We hope they make your own critics seem a little less bothersome. (Please note that in the interest of keeping the peace—what little there may be between the parents and their critics—we're not using names in this section.)

- "My mother-in-law just kept badgering me. My husband wouldn't stand up to her. She kept on attacking me until I blew up and wouldn't speak to her. She finally shamed me into letting our baby cry it out. I put him in a crib and let him cry. 'He's spoiled,' she would chant. 'He'll quit soon,' she would assure me. I just couldn't take it anymore. I went up, against her restraints, and picked him up. He was burning up with fever and had vomited all over the room. I never did that again with any of my children."

  —A MOTHER OF FOUR CHILDREN, AGES TEN TO ONE

- "My mom was always saying, 'It'll make your child a pervert.'"

  —A MOTHER OF THREE, WHO IS HAPPY TO REPORT
  THAT HER CHILDREN ARE MOSTLY DONE WITH
  THE FAMILY BED AND "ARE WONDERFUL,
  WELL-ADJUSTED, AND NONPERVERTED"

- "My brother challenged me in the middle of a family party and asked me in front of everyone where my husband and I had sex."

  —A MOTHER OF A TWO-YEAR-OLD GIRL

- Baby's grandmother: "You can choose to do anything else you want however you want to do it ... but if you kill my grandchild by smothering him to death how could you live with yourself?"

  Baby's step-grandfather, angry, calling immediately after grandmother hangs up the phone: "Do you realize what you are making your mother go through? Enough of this nonsense already!"

Good Nights

Baby's mother: "My family freaked out when they found out he was in the bed with me. I got phone calls for days on end that I was going to kill my baby by smothering him to death. I even called my doctor to ask if that was true, and he said no. He said it was fine to have the baby in bed with me. My family was unrelenting and came over and set up the crib for me and browbeat me into using it. I was a new young mom and was very vulnerable."

—A MOTHER OF TWO YOUNG BOYS. SHE LATER DISCOVERED
THE CRIB WASN'T EVEN UP TO SAFETY CODE

- "My mother-in-law pressures my husband to force me to change our sleep setup, and she badmouths our family bed to all the relatives on his side of the family."

—A MOTHER OF A TWENTY-TWO-MONTH-OLD GIRL

- "My family doctor referred me to a psychiatrist who tried his hardest to persuade me to take medication to control my 'unnatural anxiety' about wanting my newborn with me at night. I adamantly refused.... By the time we settled into the family bed situation, my husband and I had questioned my sanity, instincts, and judgment. It took a lot of dedication and research on my part to convince both of us that my desire was normal and natural and, in fact, healthy."

—A FIRST-TIME MOTHER WHO FINALLY
BROUGHT HER DAUGHTER INTO BED
AFTER SEVEN MONTHS OF STRUGGLING TO
CONFORM TO "NORMS" AND PRESSURES

DR. JAY: *It's my opinion that this was medical malpractice.*

- "My mother-in-law is so appalled that we'd have Jilly in our bed that she has stopped communicating with us. She refuses to talk to us again until we're done 'being stupid' and 'warping our child.' It's sad because she's losing out on her granddaughter and vice-versa. On the other hand, who needs relatives like this?"

    —A MOTHER OF AN EIGHTEEN-MONTH-OLD GIRL

Critical Survival Tools

An important tool to possess for coping with criticism is a deep confidence in what you're doing. (An added benefit of confidence is that the more confident you are, the less guff you're likely to get—and the less you're likely to take, too!)

But since most people can't just wake up one morning and truly change their outlook by saying, "Starting today, I'm going to be confident," we bring you some suggestions that will help you feel positively unflappable:

Rally the Troops: Surround yourself with supportive people. Having other family bedders to talk with (or even just e-mail) can be invaluable. "Finding someone else who co-slept was my life raft," says Cheryl, a mother of two young girls (see "Helpful Resources," page 195, for how to hook up with other family parents, or at least those who support the family bed).

Don't Blabber About Bed: If you're sensitive
to criticism, you may want to be careful who you tell about
your family bed. Too many mothers have approached other
parents at the playground and started discussing their sleeping
arrangements in hopes that the other parents might also be
family bedders. This can backfire, with the other parents being
avidly against co-sleeping and not hesitating to say so. There
are better ways to find like-minded parents.

Know You Aren't Alone: Even though you
may feel like the only person on this planet who shares a bed
with a baby, you are far from alone. In fact, most people on
earth co-sleep. Even in the United States, many more people
co-sleep than you'd ever suspect. Don't look now, but you
know that neighbor who doesn't talk much about how her
baby sleeps? She just may be a closet co-sleeper. (Did you ever
wonder why her baby's crib was always so spotless? Almost
as though no one ever slept in it, eh?) There are many out there
like her. Oh, and did we tell you how most of the rest of the
world sleeps yet? See "Around the World in Forty Winks,"
page 137.

Know the Facts: The more knowledge you have
about co-sleeping, the better off you'll be. Whether you use it
solely to bolster your confidence or you brandish your knowledge when the critics come on too strong, knowing the science
and the stories—both positive and negative—behind co-sleeping
will prove immensely helpful.

Know Where They're Coming From:
Try to understand that your critics probably don't understand. They may even mean well. But as Dan, a father of three, says, "They have social momentum and old habits on their side."

Defer to the Doctor: (A note from Dr. Jay)
You'll be amazed how much it helps when you bring a doctor into the picture. Feel free to use me. I don't mind a bit if you need to tell a family bed critic that the pediatrician says co-sleeping is best. Critics don't have to know that the pediatrician is not necessarily your child's pediatrician, right?

Look to the Graduates: People who spent time
in the family bed as children are some of the most wonderful, well-adjusted folks around. See what we say about them in chapter 1 and what they say about themselves and their childhoods in chapter 8.

Look to Your Baby: Isn't it amazing that with all
the criticism you get about co-sleeping, your baby is still the favorite of so many people? Much of this is your child's inborn temperament, of course, but we think at least some stems from your child's most important needs being met, day and night. All that cuddling and snuggling tends to make a happy baby.

Make 'Em Laugh: If you're in the mood, try using
humor to deflect some criticism. You'll find that well-placed humor can not only ease a tense situation, but can actually transform your critic's views of co-sleeping. An example of a fun retort to a commonly asked question:

Q: So, when are you going to make them sleep in their own beds?

A: Well, it depends on if [insert college of your choice here] has single or double beds in the dorms.
(Thanks to Magdalena, mother of three family bed kids, for this one.)

Make 'Em Blush: If you're talking with someone whose rudeness has exceeded all reasonable bounds, it may help to point out their boorishness. A good response to an embarrassing or too-personal inquiry: "That's an extremely personal question. I'm surprised you'd be so [fill in the blank: rude/unkind/impolite/nosy/brazen]." That should be the last you hear from them about the subject.

Nod Off: Practice nodding your head in front of the mirror. Say, "Yes, I think you may have a point. I'll have to consider that," and other amicable statements, with a smile on your face. This way, when you find yourself in the hands of a disapproving critic and you don't feel like explaining your reasons for co-sleeping, you'll be well-versed at a pleasant front.

Mother/Father Knows Best: Realize that as your child's parents, you're probably the best judges of what's right for your family. Your neighbors, your friends, and even your parents don't know your family and your situation the way you do.

Choose Your Battles: Knowing which battles to fight and which to gracefully refuse to enter can make your life a lot easier. This comes with experience, but you'd be wise to choose not to go all-out with a mere acquaintance or a stranger.

Look Down the Road a Bit: Remember when in doubt: Will it really matter in twenty years what others think of where your baby slept? (And in some cases, will you even remember the names of some of the loudest critics?)

Sadly, we know of many parents who—decades after letting someone pressure them into banning a child from the bed or forcing a baby to cry it out—still have regrets. A mother of six grown children related this story: "One day my mother kept insisting that I was ruining my son (number five) with all the nursing and sleeping together. He was about a year or so old. She opened up a portable crib and moved him in so he'd fall asleep on his own. I sat on the edge of my mattress as he cried his eyes out inches from me, arms extended. As soon as my mother walked out, I picked him up and nursed him. It is twenty-one years later that I am writing this. It might as well be minutes later. I can still feel our pain, the sadness of the experience."

Relive the Bliss: Remember how deep-in-your-heart happy you feel when you wake up in the morning next to your sweet baby, or when you're snuggled up beside her at night? Try to retain that feeling and carry it out into the world when you face people who might try to pull you down.

"Oh, when my girls are snuggled up to me at bedtime, that moment alone makes things really clear to me," says Tica, mother of two young girls. "It helps me know what I am doing is right."

Use Star Power

When a man like Pierce Brosnan (who portrays a recent and very popular James Bond) refers to books that are against co-sleeping as "completely cracked" and admits he loves sharing a bed with his baby,[1] it can help make the family bed a little more acceptable. (After all, if James Bond can share a bed with a baby, who can't?)

Sometimes, a little name-dropping can go a long way toward making others realize how widespread co-sleeping has become. This alone can help deflect criticism of those who see it as a "fringey" thing to do. With this in mind, we bring you a few famous folks who co-slept, either as children or parents.

A NOTE FROM DR. JAY: *Because of the neighborhood I work in, I have an awful lot of high-profile parents whose children are my patients. They are movie stars, directors, politicians, you name it. Many dozens use the family bed. But out of respect for their privacy, I won't be divulging any of their names. The people you'll read about here are those who have already had their stories told in books, magazines, and on television.*

- Writer Maya Angelou, as a parent. (For her own description of her first night co-sleeping, see page 51.)
- Academy Award–winning actor Roberto Benigni. As a child, he shared a bed with a parent and three siblings. (Which he agreed was "wonderful" when asked by *60 Minutes* reporter Bob Simon.)[2]

  With his usual bright outlook on life, Benigni told *People* magazine about a time when his very poor family slept in a friend's stable separated from a horse by one plank of wood for three weeks. "There was this face of a horse that we would see in the night looking at us from up high," the comic actor recalled. "It was beautiful—a bit like Jesus in the stall. It was fantastic sleeping there."[3]
- Mick Jagger and Jerry Hall, as parents, with at least one of their children. (Although reports are that Jagger wasn't necessarily thrilled by the length of the arrangement.)[4]
- Singer-songwriter Kenny Loggins, as a parent. He even showed a reporter from *Home & Garden Television* his luxurious master bedroom, complete with an enormous beautiful family bed.[5]
- Sophia Loren, as a child.[6]
- Elvis Presley, as a child.[7]

Set the Story Straight

You may decide to educate someone who's throwing you the old myths about co-sleeping. The guide below gives seven of the most common erroneous comments about the family bed, and the pages of this book where you can find the myth-busting facts. Consider it a family bed crib sheet (so to speak).

- "He won't learn independence."—Nonsense! Allowing dependence in the early months and years increases independence later in life because the child has a strong foundation (see chapter 1, pages 23–27).

- "She'll turn out weird."—Mamma mia! (See chapter 1, pages 21–23, and the words from family bed "graduates" in chapter 8.)

- "You'll suffocate him."—There are safety guidelines for everything, even co-sleeping (see chapter 3).

- "She'll never leave your bed."—Wrong, although it *might* take awhile (see chapter 7).

- "It'll wreck your marriage and sex life!"—Quite the opposite, if you put a little effort into things (see chapter 5).

- "You have to let her cry it out in the crib. It's the only way she'll learn to sleep."—Since when do humans need sleep schooling? (See chapter 4, pages 93–104, for a look at cry-it-out sleep-training techniques. Also see chapter 1 and "Sleeping Like a Baby," page 84, for more on "natural" infant sleep.)

- "Only hippies and poor people do that!"—Hey, man, that is like *so* wrong! Eighty percent of breast-feeding mothers in our culture co-sleep (see page 14). So does most of the rest of the world. (See "Around the World in Forty Winks," below.) And in case you're interested, just about any animal that cares for its young does, too. (See "Birds Do It, Beasts Do It" page 92.)

Around the World in Forty Winks

"This child co-sleeps with her two brothers because Italian people love to sleep together always."
—ITALIAN MOTHER TO AMERICAN SLEEP RESEARCHERS[6]

Tonight, on beds, mats, and hammocks around the world, babies and toddlers from all walks (and crawls) of life—from the few remaining hunter-gatherer societies to non-industrial cultures to powerful industrial nations like Japan—will be sleeping next to parents or other caretakers.

Around the globe, babies—and even toddlers—rarely sleep alone. The United States and several Western European countries are the exceptions when it comes to the global perspective on where their young should sleep.*

---

*Of course, no country is homogeneous. Different cultures within a country are bound to differ in their child-rearing practices.

In a study of 186 nonindustrial societies, not one society let a baby under one year sleep alone.[9] (In many of these societies, co-sleeping goes until weaning from breast-feeding, or longer.) "Co-sleeping is routine in most other cultures," notes another study that compared how children in the U.S. and other countries sleep.[10]

Parents in these cultures often express shock, sadness, and pity when they learn how families in the U.S. handle their babies and young children at bedtime.[11,12] In a study comparing the sleeping arrangements of Highland Mayan parents and middle-class U.S. parents, researchers found that Mayan parents "regarded the practice of having infants and toddlers sleep in separate rooms as tantamount to child neglect."[13] Likewise, other researchers conclude that "the historically evolved behavioral script calling for nighttime separation of children from parents ... is often perceived by adults in Africa, Asia, and Central America as a form of 'child neglect.'"[14]

As one Vietnamese mother succinctly put it: "Babies are too important to be left alone with nobody watching them."[15]

Contrary to popular belief, lack of space is not often the reason for this early childhood closeness. Parents around the world have told us this. Other studies have confirmed it. Here's a smattering of what they have to say:

- "Westerners viewing Japanese sleeping arrangements usually sense a high degree of 'overcrowding,' which they say results from lack of space in 'densely populated' Japan. We argue that this apparent 'overcrowding' in the bedroom is only part a function of lack of space: It derives more directly from the strength of family bonds . . . the frequency with which children co-sleep with parents expresses a strong cultural emphasis upon the nurturant aspects of family life."

—FROM A STUDY ABOUT CO-SLEEPING IN JAPAN[16]

• "Even very wealthy, powerful families share a bed with children because it is a matter of parenting style . . . it's a matter of culture in that family is the most important element in life."

—LORY, A MOTHER FROM THE PHILIPPINES

• "Infants commonly slept in the same rooms as their parents regardless of the availability of separate sleeping rooms. It was considered unkind to put an infant to sleep alone in a room."

—FROM A FIELD STUDY OF ITALIAN BABY CARE[17]

• "The lack of space does not determine if children share a bed . . . Cribs are rarely used in Zimbabwe . . . Personally, I think of them as little jails."

—A MOTHER (WHO WISHED TO REMAIN ANONYMOUS) FROM AN INDIAN COMMUNITY IN ZIMBABWE

In most cultures where co-sleeping is commonplace, parents rely on grandparents and other elder family and community members for child-rearing guidance. In contrast, parents in the United States—where nuclear families and lack of close extended family are the norm—have a long history of relying on "scientific" recommendations on child rearing.[18] (One of these expert recommendations, as you may recall, was for mothers to abandon breast-feeding in favor of bottle-feeding. We now know how sound that advice was.)

Unfortunately, the siren song of affluent Western countries often tempts people in other countries to copy our ways. From what several respondents to our special international co-sleeping questionnaire tell us, cribs are starting to show up more in countries where they were once rare.

"As [Hong Kong] society has become richer and been more influenced by the West, more children have been moved into their own beds, and babies often have cribs," says a Hong Kong transport engineer and family bed father of three. "But it still seems easy for them to return to the parent's bed. [It's] almost as though the space has arrived before the attitude."

We can only hope that Western attitudes change before the worldwide bed becomes a lot less inviting for babies.

7.

A Farewell to Arms—
and Legs . . . and Feet . . .
Moving Beyond the Family Bed

ZZZZZZZZZZZZZZZZ

You've stroked his downy hair as he dreamed his first baby dreams in your arms. You've clung to the edge of the bed while his little body somehow took up all the room. You've slept your sweetest sleep while he nestled so cozily in your arms. And you've barely caught a wink while sleep transformed him into a future World Cup soccer star.

Now comes a bittersweet time. Your little one wants his own bed. Or you'd like him to start moving in that direction.

For some, the transition is quick and simple. The child says he'd rather sleep in his room by himself one night, and he's off. (Yes, it really does happen this way with some kids.)

For others, it takes time.

On days when it seems like your child will never leave the family bed, it can help to keep this in mind: Your child really will leave! The transition out may not come as early as you'd imagined when you first brought your newborn into bed. (Trust us, your baby won't be covetously eyeing his crib at seven months, wishing he could just sleep all alone instead of with loving parents.) But your child will be sleeping on his own soon enough. The time goes so fast, and the nights he spends snuggling next to you will be but a blink—at least in hindsight.

But just how does a child whose greatest love is sleeping next to warm and adoring parents actually end up willing and able to sleep without them? It depends on the child, on family dynamics, on parental philosophies, even on the setup of the house. Believe it or not, there are as many ways for a child to leave the family bed as there are ways for a child to enter the bed in the first place!

Some parents are purists, not wanting to influence their child's departure from the bed at all. Others believe in gently helping a child move on when they feel the time is right for everyone.

We now bring you a plethora of ideas, much practical advice, and, we hope, something that will work for you and your family when the time comes for your child to move beyond the family bed.

Paws to Reflect

More than 60 percent of Americans allow their pets to sleep in bed with them on a regular basis, according to an extensive national survey.[1] If only our babies were lucky enough to be treated like the majority of our pets!

In Their Own Time

The purist philosophy about weaning children from co-sleeping is summed up well by one phrase: "Leave them alone 'til they leave on their own."

Many parents swear by it, and it can work beautifully if you're in no hurry to move your child out of your bed. It's like child-led weaning from the breast. There are no enticements to move on—it's all on the child's timetable.

Since children in the family bed usually love the security, the affection, the camaraderie, and the closeness that comes with sleeping there, they're not often in a rush to lay claim to their own beds. Kids given the freedom to wean from the family bed with little or no parental influence tend to be significantly older than children whose parents take even a slightly more active role in transitioning them out of bed. It's not uncommon for six year olds to still be co-sleeping when parents go this route.

"We were beginning to wonder if Sam was ever going to sleep on his own, and it happened so unexpectedly," says family bed mom Carol. "The day he turned six, he said he was a big boy now and that he was ready for his own bed. And boom, that was it! It was so easy."

Parents don't always have to wait so long for a child to decide to leave on his own. We know dozens of parents whose children started hankering for their own beds when they were about four years old. Several left on their own around two or three. And a few children have really floored their parents by opting for their own beds when they were barely able to walk.

Good Nights

At fifteen months old, little Dodi toddled to her own room one night and plaintively wailed, "Dere! I night-night dere!" until her parents realized that she wanted to sleep in her own room by herself. She slept through the night on the futon on the floor from that night on.

Then there's the other end of the calendar, when a child ends up in the family bed for a very long time. It's vary rare in our culture, but we've heard from a few families where children were in bed until puberty. (An important note: This almost always happens when parents do nothing to help their children transition into another bed at some point. A little help with the transition, and children inevitably graduate much earlier.)

Lynn, a family bed mom of six grown children, remembers her own childhood in the family bed very clearly: She was thirteen when she finally left—the oldest of any of the American family bedders we've heard from. "I loved the warmth and closeness," she says. But one day she started thinking about boys in a new way "and suddenly I was horrified and embarrassed about sleeping in my parents' bed." She began sleeping in her own room immediately and never looked back.

Lynn went on to lead a normal, happy, successful life. She says her extra time in the family bed did her no harm and probably helped make her a very compassionate person. The only aspect of her thirteen-year stay she questions is how it may have affected her parents' relationship.

Having a child in your bed for many years probably won't harm your relationship with your partner as long as you're both in agreement on the situation and you find/make time to be alone together. But when one parent wants to let a child stay in bed as long as the child wants, and the other doesn't, it can put a serious strain on the relationship.

We can't overstate the importance of a harmonious parental relationship. We'd rather see a three year old gently helped to get used to his own bed than a marriage split up because he's in it. Parents at odds over an older child in bed need to take a serious look at the problem and do whatever it takes to come to a decision everyone can live with.

In some cases nature has been known to pull some miracles that even the best marriage counselors couldn't accomplish.

"Our son . . . showed no signs of leaving our bed," says "Mike," who asked that his real name not be used. "I'd been very tolerant for years, but I was coming to the end of my rope. My wife wouldn't budge about helping him move to his own bed, and I was feeling like eight years was more than enough time in bed with him."

Fortunately for everyone, Mike's wife became pregnant (they had a guest room down the hall for intimate encounters). When the baby was born, the girl became a family bedder. With four in the bed—one of them more noisy than the others—Mike's son decided it was time to head out. Three years later his little sister joined him in his room. "Our daughter probably saved our marriage," says Mike.

A new baby is actually the biggest reason family bed kids make a beeline for their own beds. If you want to stick with the child-led transition concept, you may need do nothing more than simply have another baby for your other child to decide to sleep on his own.

Of course, there are less dramatic ways for you to inspire your child to bounce into his own bed. The next section will provide you with plenty of ideas along these lines.

A Nurturing Nudge

Just as some birds give their babies a gentle bump to help them leave the nest, some family bed parents give their children a nurturing nudge to help them leave the family bed.

The reasons parents want a child to move on vary greatly. They may feel the child is getting too old for co-sleeping. They may want to reclaim their own bed. They may need a calmer sleeping arena. Some have a partner who objects to co-sleeping. Many need the space because a new baby is on the way.

Whatever your reason for wanting your child to graduate to a bed of his own, helping him move on to the next stage of his night life is a natural progression, an extension of the tender nighttime parenting you've been practicing all along. Do it with compassion and patience, observing your child's reactions and taking the time to find out what works for him, and you and your child will be rewarded with a comfortable transition.

But push your child out of the nest too abruptly or too hard, and you're likely to ruffle some feathers. Children forced out in this manner can become clingy and may end up back in bed with you for an extended period. This is particularly true with children who are temperamentally inclined to be sensitive to separation in the first place. You have to know your child, know what he might handle well, what might make him miserable. If you feel feel he's really not ready for the separation, and you're not in a hurry for him to leave, wait a bit. A little more time in the family bed can help make the transition much easier.

A NOTE FROM DR. JAY: *Some of the unhappiest people I have seen are parents who moved their child out of bed too early because of pressure from other people. If it's truly your decision and you want to wean your child from bed, you'll be OK. But bow to coercion before you think the time is right, and you may regret it.*

One of the most frequent questions we're asked is about the best age to wean a child from the family bed. While the optimal weaning age varies from child to child, many children can segue out fairly easily starting when they're two or three years old.

That's the age when children are beginning to enjoy their growing independence from their parents. Children this age have developed an entrenched sense of object permanence (the ability to remember and create a mental image of an object or person they can't see). This means they can maintain the sense of security that comes with the presence of a parent, even when the parent is not immediately present. Children start exploring farther away from parents, needing less of the reassurance they get from keeping them in immediate view.

In addition, two year olds, flush with their capacities for movement, thought, and language, often push for autonomy. (Although admittedly, not often at night.) Parents can sometimes capitalize on that thrust and help them launch into more independent sleep situations. But if you want to wait a little longer, it's much easier with three year olds. They're capable of abstract reasoning and can understand much more complex ideas than two year olds.

But just because a child may be starting to feel more independent in certain ways doesn't necessarily mean he's ready to sleep on his own. Bedtime can be sacred to family bed children, and for some, no amount of coaxing at this age will pry them out of the family bed.

Some children have an older ideal weaning age. When they're ready, the transition often happens quite quickly and painlessly. We've heard quotes like this from plenty of parents of children this age: "We just said X and did Y, and suddenly he was sleeping in his own bed. It was so easy!"

At the other age extreme are babies. Some parents start the family bed for survival purposes but never intended to do it for long, and start looking for a way out when the baby is just months old. While ideally we'd like to see parents wait until the child is older, we can't condemn their desire to wean their baby from bed before the perfect time for the child: These parents have already given their infant a great gift. Even a few months in the family bed can get a baby off to a healthier and happier start than if the baby had slept solo all along.

Weaning a baby from the family bed often proves difficult to the baby and the parents. But some babies *can* leave with little fuss. If a child sleeps long and strong, he can transition to the crib fairly happily as early as a few months of age. Babies who aren't champion sleepers can also potentially be weaned from the bed without trauma, but it won't be as easy.

What follows is a cornucopia of tried-and-true bed-weaning tips. The first group of tips are for children who are two years and older, although some of the tips can work for slightly younger children. The second list of tips focuses on a few compassionate ways to help a baby move out of the family bed.

Whatever your child's age, use care when selecting a weaning method. Some may be perfect for your child. Others will make him cling to your bed like a fitted sheet. You may find that a combination of tips works best for your child. If none of our myriad suggestions fits your child, we hope you'll at least find some inspiration in the list to help you tailor your own plan.

Keep in mind that you'll need to make sure your house is nice and safe for your child once he's out of your bed. In the family bed, he may not have been able to get out without your knowledge, but in his own bed, the house is his to explore. Make sure every area he has access to is childproofed.

A final note: Be prepared for any reaction. The transition from bed often becomes a work in progress, with a little separation here, a little more togetherness there, a big step out of bed, a little hop back into it. But the transition can also be so quick it may leave you in shock.

"I'm still getting used to the empty space," says Claire, a Michigan mom of a three-year-old girl who left for her own room as soon as her teddy bear "told" her he'd like to sleep there with her. "If I'd have known she'd go that fast, I think I'd have made Theo keep his mouth shut for a couple more months."

Eighteen Terrific
Transition Tips

First from the Breast, then from the Nest: Weaning from the family bed usually goes much more smoothly if a child first weans from nighttime nursing. Once no longer breast-feeding at night, your child will likely wake up less frequently, which will make it easier for him to get through the night on his own.

We don't encourage weaning a child from the breast at night just to accomplish the transition from the bed. But the breast-then-nest sequence is something to keep in mind when it comes to timing your attempt to wean your child from the family bed.

(That said, in some cases, children have done very well sleeping in their own beds before weaning from the breast. By virtue of the fact that they weren't bumping against the milk factory all night, they ended up sleeping for longer periods than they may have in the family bed. This in turn helped them wean from the breast.)

Plant the Seed: Many children love looking forward to things they'll do when they're a little older. For instance, "What will I do when I'm four?" is a frequent question out of the mouths of three year olds. If your child is inquisitive about the future, you may want to take advantage of his curiosity and mention, among other activities, that he'll be sleeping in his very own bed/in a futon next to mommy and daddy/whatever you'd like the next weaning step to be. If you mention it occasionally in a positive, enthusiastic way, your child can come to see having his own bed as a very "big-kid" event to look forward to. This technique has also been successful with weaning children from pacifiers and even from breast-feeding. (Of course if the news of the new bed makes your child miserable, drop this strategy for a while. We know one little boy who refused to have a birthday party because he knew he'd stop co-sleeping on his next birthday.)

If your child turns out not to be ready for the transition at the given milestone, don't force it. Ask him when he thinks he'd be ready for his own bed, and if you think it's appropriate, try it again.

If You Build It, They Will Come: Simply providing your child with a bed or room to call his own, and then introducing him to it, may be all it takes for your child to move out of the family bed. This can even work for the younger set. "He immediately liked having his own bed," says family bed dad Dan, about his eldest son, who was twenty months old when he moved to his own room. "He went right to it the very first night and has been back with us only two or three times." (Many children leave the family bed after moving to a new house. See the "Or a Fresh Start" tip on page 163 for more on this.)

A Little Something on the Side: A gentle and highly effective way to ease your child from the family bed is to get him his very own bed and place it flush up against your bed. A new bed makes a great birthday present for a two year old. (Throw in some fun new sheets while you're at it.)

Good Nights

Children this age are starting to feel the tug of independence, but may not yet be ready to pull themselves far from their parents.

It's wise to provide a child in this situation with a twin bed, rather than a toddler bed. A twin bed has the advantage of fitting your growing child much longer than a toddler bed and also fitting next to the family bed better; you may be able to match the height of your bed and the twin bed exactly. This comes in handy for comfort and ease of a parent moving from one bed to the other for storytime, nursing, or snuggling.

When the beds are the same height, you have only a crack to contend with, rather than the Grand Canyon. If your beds don't initially match in height, you may be able to make adjustments. One family even added an extra futon on top of their girl's box spring and mattress and frame so it was as tall as their top mattress. "She looked a bit like the princess and the pea, but she slept a lot better than her," says her mom. (Be sure to follow the appropriate safety precautions, including adding a guardrail if the other side of the bed isn't against the wall, when setting up the new bed.)

Children and parents usually view the twin bed as more than an extension of the family bed. "It's her bed. She talks about her 'big-girl bed' all the time," says Frank, of his twenty-six-month-old daughter. "We also consider it her bed. We take less heat from our relatives now that they know she has her own bed. Of course, they don't necessarily know how close it is to ours."

Some parents wait until their child is ready (it may take a few months, it may take much longer), and then start moving the child's bed a little farther from the family bed every so often (don't forget a guardrail on the newly exposed side!). Eventually the bed, like a local-stop train, ends up at its terminus—usually the child's room. Other parents just wait until their children are ready to take the express route to the final destination. "One day, after two years in her twin bed beside us, Emma asked if she could move it into her own room," says Vanessa, of her five-year-old daughter. "It was easier than easy, and it was a sweet transition for us all."

Look Out Below: An alternative to the setup in the previous tip is to place a futon or mattress on the floor of your room either beside you or at the foot of your bed for your child's first venture out of the family bed. It's safe (just don't step on him) and it's relatively inexpensive. Some children take the transition in stride, not being bothered that they're no longer at the same level as their parents. "I liked it because I wasn't as close, but I was close," says a ten-year-old girl who left the family bed for a futon when she was five. Many children still need to be parented to sleep for a while during the transition to the new sleeping arrangement.

(Allergy alert: Go low only if you're willing to keep the floor area very clean. Dust mites, who make a living on dust, are big allergens, and increase the chances of asthma.)

Bank on Bunks: And now for the tallest—and many think the best—beds for your child's transition out of the family bed: bunk beds. Kids love bunk beds. They've proven to be the magical answer to many a parent's bed-weaning worries.

"I thought Jill would be stuck beside me in bed forever. She showed no signs of being able to leave," says Leslie, of her four-year-old family bedder. "Then one night we stayed somewhere that had bunks, and she announced she would be sleeping alone that night. I thought, *Ya, right.* She climbed the ladder, said good night, and played with a stuffed animal until I saw her little arm dangling through the guard rail. She slept through the night up there every night during our stay." Back home, Leslie and her husband headed straight for a furniture store and bought bunk beds. Jill has been happily sleeping in the top bunk ever since. An only child, she uses the bottom bunk for sleepovers and dolls.

For safety reasons, children should be at least four before sleeping in the top bed of most bunks. Designs differ, and minimum safe ages may vary, so inquire before you buy.

Here's a hint if you want to check out your child's reaction to sleeping in bunk beds before investing in them: Stay at a KOA Kamping Kabin for a night or two. These cozy, country-style log cabins are located at KOA campgrounds throughout the United States. Each comes with at least one queen-sized bed and a bunk bed. (The Ritz it's not, though. It's more like camping indoors. There's no bathroom inside, and you bring your own bedding. But it can be great family fun.)

Send Them to a Sib: The idea of sleeping in the same room as an older brother or sister is so tantalizing to some children that the transition from the family bed is seamless and pain free. The child simply leaves his parents to sleep with another loved one rather than alone. Moving in with an older sibling is one of the most common ways children around the globe wean from the parental bed—and also one of the easiest and most enjoyable. It's *Leave It to Beaver* all over again, with Wally and the Beav sharing a room and a big part of their lives. Even the affluent, with an abundance of rooms, often put same-sex children in the same bedroom, at least for a while.

Surprisingly, older siblings are generally happy to have a

little companion near them at night. "My oldest would read to his little brother. Sometimes they would get goofy and play around, but I remember watching them and being so over-whelmed with warmth and love," says family bed mom Lysa of her little boy's time in his big brother's bed.

Lysa's youngest boy made the move into his own bed shortly after transitioning to his brother's bed. That's also a common scenario with children who have older siblings: They have an example of another child sleeping alone, and they may strive for that same independence.

Of course sleeping next to a younger sibling is not always a bed of roses. Occasionally it turns out to be a bed of wetness: "My oldest daughter still remembers waking up for high school and finding out that my youngest daughter had wet the bed. (She wore a diaper to bed, but it had leaked.)," recalls Janet, mom of four family bed children.

Not all older children will react well to a younger sibling moving in with them. If you have the luxury of space, don't force the issue if your older child objects strenuously or doesn't normally enjoy the company of his younger sibling. In addition, don't move a baby in with a sibling. Sleeping children may not be aware of a baby's presence in bed, and it could be hazardous for the baby.

Or Let a Sib Send Them: The number-one rea-son children leave the family bed is because of the arrival of a new baby in the bed, according to our questionnaires and interviews. It's amazing how many children willingly—and happily—head for their own beds after a few days or weeks of bunking with baby. "One week after the baby's birth, Brit asked if she could sleep in her own room," says Sylvie of her

two-and-a half-year-old daughter, who had once told her mom she never wanted to leave the family bed. "You could have knocked me over with a feather."

So if you're pregnant and trying without success to wean your child from the family bed, you might want to relax and let nature take its course. Your child could well pack out on his own shortly after your baby's birth.

Having another baby is no guarantee, however, that your child will suddenly move on. We've heard from several families whose children love sharing the family bed with their new siblings. In fact, some of these families ended up with three or four children in the bed at once (they modified the bed situation a bit) before someone decided to move to another bed. "It was legs and arms and happy sleepy faces everywhere," says Mary, who remembers this "puppy" stage fondly. (We go over a few comfort and safety tips for expanding family beds in chapter 4, page 91.)

A final note: Not that infrequently, a child who has been sleeping well in his own bed suddenly wants to be back in the family bed when a new baby takes up residency there. For your child's sake, it's best not to fight the relocation too hard. He'll move on again when he's ready. "Actually, I prefer her here now," says a mom whose three-year-old daughter rejoined the family bed after twin siblings were born. "Since the twins came along, I have less time to spend with her during the day, so sleeping together helps us reconnect at night."

Play Musical Beds: Children making the transition out of the family bed don't always start the night where they end it. In fact a bit of bed-hopping is often part of a healthy, humane bed-weaning scenario. Here are the two main ways your child (and you!) may end up playing musical beds:

1. **Start the night apart and let your child join you when he wakes:** Read to your child, nurse him, or do whatever it takes to get him comfortable in his own bed. Many parents stay with their children until they fall asleep. (The children, that is, not the parents—although this often ends up happening, too.) Alternatively, if your child is ready for it, he can start the night alone with a minimum of nighttime parenting.

Then if your child wakes up before morning and is unhappy/can't get back to sleep on his own, he can join you in the family bed. Make it clear that the door is always open. Most children in this situation are very considerate when they join you in bed; "She's very quiet," says Tess about her occasional five-year-old visitor. "I'm not usually even aware of when she gets into our bed."

It helps if your room happens to be close to your child's. We've known of a couple of kids who were so sleepy they couldn't negotiate the way to their parents' room. "We found him under his dresser a couple of times in the middle of the night," says Judith, whose three-and-a-half-year-old son apparently started the trip to his parents' room but couldn't quite make it.

2. **Start the night together, then move your child:** Here's almost the direct opposite of the last method. Your child starts the night in the family bed as usual. After he's asleep, you carry him to his own bed. (Note: This works better with children who won't give you a hernia upon lifting them.)

Be sure to explain this plan to your child ahead of time so he's not completely confused when he wakes up in a different place. As he gets more used to the move, he'll likely become more comfortable when he wakes up. As with the previous "musical bed" technique, if your child wakes up unhappy during the night, he should feel free to rejoin you in the family bed.

Many families find that gradually doing this brings the best results. You may want to try moving your child only a couple of nights a week at first, then three or four nights, then every night. "Most nights now they just lie down in their bed and fall asleep on their own," says LaJuana whose four year old and six year old gradually weaned into their own bed in this manner.

Will the Real Family Bedders Please Stand Up?

We all know that plenty of parents are dead set against the family bed. But ironically, millions of these very same parents practice co-sleeping on a nightly basis.

They just don't realize they're doing it.

The majority of unwitting co-sleepers start the night with the kids sleeping in their own beds. Then at a certain point during the night, the children amble to the parents' bed, and everyone snoozes together until morning.

"It's so frustrating," says a Seattle family bed mom. "When I visit my sister and her husband, they pretty much persecute me for sharing a bed with my baby. It makes my blood boil.

"But it's so contradictory: My niece and nephew actually spend most of the night in their parents' bed. I guess my sister figures it's OK since her kids sleep a couple of hours in their own beds to start the night."

When Dr. Jay was doing a show about the family bed on ABC, there was a censor checking things out because at the time it was a topic considered too far from the absolute middle of American parenting. The discussion with the censor revealed that she had a family bed and didn't even know it! "Well," she said, "the kids have always tended to crawl into bed with us in the early morning." "Six o'clock?" he asked. "Well, more like three or four o'clock." "Oh," he said, and said no more.

Most anti-co-sleeping parents would never admit to having a family bed—not even a modified family bed. But to this we say, a rose by any other name would still smell as sweet. If the children benefit, who cares about nomenclature?

Entice Them to Exit: Ballerina pillowcases. A new puppy to share the bed. Glow-in-the-dark planets on the ceiling. A Winnie-the-Pooh comforter. Big-kid pajamas. A star projector. A yellow bed shaped like a car.

These are just some of the enticements family bed parents have successfully used to help their children feel more at home in their own beds or rooms. "I never thought a princess drape (mosquito netting) over my daughter's bed would get her out of ours," says Julie, whose four-year-old daughter had never shown any interest in her own room until the bed became regally cloaked. "It's amazing what seven yards of fabric did for us."

Some families don't limit the enticements to the bedroom. Allen, sixteen, remembers his parents' parting gift: "My parents think they bribed me out of the bed with a Super Nintendo. But I considered it more of a celebration present, like a rite of passage gift, not a bribe." Whatever they called it, it did the trick.

Not to rain on our own parade, but you may not want to invest too much in these enticements. They can work wonders for some families, but in reality, many family bed children don't go for them. Family bed kids usually much prefer the company of their parents to the lure of a material object. As Jan, a mother of four former family bedders put it, "My children knew better than to think a thing would make a difference—only a person."

But if your child is on the brink of moving out of your bed and is enamored, say, with the Flintstones, a set of Flintstones sheets and a poster of Dino just may be the catalyst for his move. Yabadabadoo!

Try a Fresh Coat: For some children, changing the decor of their bedroom can mean the difference between remaining in the family bed or striking out on their own. "We decorated his room and made it special for him, and then he didn't want to sleep in our room any longer," says Sue, about her three-year-old boy's move, which was based on a little paint and some new furniture.

Children who help participate in making decisions about how to "fix up" their room seem to be more inclined to want to move in. "She begged us to paint the room pink and to get shelves for all her dolls and paint those pink," says Neil, whose two-year-old daughter had a rosy sense of style. "She could barely wait 'til the paint dried to start sleeping there."

Or a Fresh Start: Not that you're going to buy a new house in order to get your child out of the family bed, but if you *are* planning on making a move, you should know that your child may well graduate from the family bed after the move—especially if your child didn't previously have his own room because of space constraints.

"When we moved from an apartment to a house, our son was very excited that he had his own room. We put a futon on the floor, and he wanted to sleep there," says Jennifer, whose boy was only eighteen months when he started sleeping in his own room for most of the night.

Even if your child had a room he didn't use in your old place, there's something about moving that inspires some kids to try their own new turf. "He thought it was cool that his room was a different shape and had a huge closet," says Peter, whose five-year-old son had never wanted to sleep in his old room. "The day we moved into this house, he moved out of our bed."

Let Their Imaginations Lead Them: Children who are strong on imagination have been known to venture out of the family bed with the help of their creative minds.

Two-and-a-half-year-old Jayne loved her myriad dolls as if they were real babies and wanted to fill the family bed with them so she could sleep with them and let them "nurse." "I encouraged her love for them but drew the line with sharing a bed with plastic arms and legs," says her mom. "I told her she would have to do that in her own bed, that there wasn't room in mommy's bed for all those babies. She happily moved out to share her bed with her babies."

And as we mentioned earlier in the chapter, one three-year-old girl with a lively imagination heeded the words of her favorite teddy bear (whose mom was his voice) when he mentioned he'd like to sleep in her own bed with her. "She thought that would be fun, because Theo the Bear wanted to do it," says her mom, Claire. That night they made a big deal of the bear and the girl sleeping in their own bed. It was the end of the family bed. "She had such fun being a big girl (that's what Theo told her she was) and snuggling under the covers with Theo. Suddenly she was asleep. So easy for her."

Turn on a Tape: A little night music can help soothe your child and smooth the transition out of the family bed. Several parents we've heard from have played their child's favorite music on a tape or CD player in the child's room when the child was learning to sleep solo.

Keep in mind that music alone won't accomplish the transition; it can just provide a calming backdrop to the process. Be sure not to substitute it for reading, nursing, or whatever other gentle nighttime nurturing you've been doing.

Light Up Their Lives: If your child sees monsters whenever you turn out the light in his room, by all means leave the light on for him. A nightlight or other dim light in your child's room can work wonders for eliminating fear of the dark. Or just leave the door open and a light on down the hall.

One family bed mom gave her four-year-old son a flash-light when he started sleeping in his own room. With it he chased off all monsters and made a glowing transition from the family bed.

Banish the Bogeyman: Avoid letting your child watch movies or videos that may scare him. One nine-year-old family bed "graduate" we know ended up sleeping in a sleeping bag on the floor of his parents' room for weeks after watching *Alien*.

Keep in mind that "scary" is in the eye of the beholder. A movie that may seem perfectly harmless to you may keep your child up worrying for hours. One four-year-old girl had a relapse and moved back into her parents' bed after watching *Snow White*. "She just couldn't get the witch image out of her head at night in her room by herself," says her mom.

Be a Good Neighbor: Many children find it easier to fall asleep in their own room when a parent is doing some-thing somewhat active in another room nearby. (A parent sleeping in a neighboring room doesn't seem to have the same comforting effect.) If your child knows you're in the next room sewing, writing, studying, folding laundry, painting, cooking, shining your golf clubs, or anything else that doesn't involve a lot of noise (using power tools, for instance, is not a great idea) he'll probably be more inclined to relax and nod off. "I remem-ber loving it that my mom would always be in her room right next to mine, folding laundry or ironing after she read to me," recalls DeeAnna, who left the family bed at five, but whose mom performed these nightly chores nearby for years. "I felt protected, lulled to sleep by her being so close and doing these 'mom' things."

Give Them a Round-Trip Ticket: It's a good idea to let your child know he's welcome to come back to your bed for a few hours or a night whenever he wants to or needs to. If your child senses that the door will slam shut behind him as soon as he attempts to venture out on his own, he'll be less likely to set a toe out of the family bed. Having an open-bed policy makes the transition easier. "They slept more comfortably knowing they could come back any time," says Niesha, mother of four children. And for parents, the transition is also less traumatic this way: "I felt like I was saying 'see you later' instead of a big, final 'good-bye,'" says Rhonda, whose two preschoolers spend a cuddly night in her bed once every couple of months.

Ways to Wean a Wee One

The following tips are for parents who have babies they'd like to move from the family bed to a crib. We recommend doing some soul-searching before you try to wean your baby out of the family bed: Do you really want to do this or are you bowing to the pressure of someone who doesn't really matter? If there's a problem in the family bed, is there anything you can do to fix it? (See chapter 4 for some help along these lines.)

If you really want to move your baby out of the family bed, try to keep your weaning techniques as gentle as your nighttime parenting style has been. While some babies transition into the crib without much fuss, the majority will not be thrilled about the move. After all, they may be little, but they know a good thing when they've got it.

It may seem impossible, but on rare occasions, it's actually the baby who wants "out": At sixteen months, little Fiona began appearing unhappy in the family bed and climbing out whenever she got a chance. "So we put up her crib and put her in it one night, and she went to sleep," says her mom. "She appeared to be very happy to have her own space. I don't think Fiona missed us at all. But we missed her a lot! It was much harder on us than on her. Dad hates it that she sleeps in the crib, and we have tried to get her into our bed just for snuggles, but she won't do it."

If your baby is begging to go, by all means let him. But for the vast majority of those with babies who want to continue to sleep close, we offer a few tips to help make the transition as woe-free as possible.

Sidle Up to a Sidecar: You can have your own space while still keeping your baby within arm's reach by using the sidecar setup we described on page 60. This way your baby has his crib (albeit a three-sided one) or sidecar bed, and you can still roll over to nurse or comfort him. Then you can scooch back to your own bed and enjoy the extra room. It's not like having the baby in a separate nursery, but it's a compassionate way to wean him from your bed. Once he's used to sleeping without feeling you all the time, it may be easier to gradually move his setup farther from the bed, if you want to take that step while he's still a baby.

Fall Asleep and Then Go to Bed: Some
parents let their baby fall asleep while they're holding or rocking or nursing the baby. They make sure the baby is in a deep
sleep, and then gently place him in the crib and let him snooze
there. (Sleep-training advocates don't like this technique
because they say a child comes to rely on a parent for falling
asleep. There's some truth to this, but we don't have a problem
with a baby relying on parents for a few essentials.)

Babies who sleep well after being placed in the crib are the
ones who have a fair chance at weaning well with this method.
Many babies will awaken while their parents are still hovering
over the crib. This plan is not for them.

Some babies will sleep for hours after you put them down,
others for fifteen minutes. Whenever your baby wakes up,
don't leave him to cry. Continue being a nurturing parent and
give him what he needs, whether it's a breast, a diaper change,
or the family bed. The first time each of Cheryl's three children
would awaken in their cribs (after being "parented down") during the night, she'd bring them into the family bed. "As they
got older," she says, "they slept longer and longer in their own
beds until they were sleeping through the night [there]."

Do It in the Daylight: If you can get your baby
used to taking naps in his crib, the transition to the crib at
night can be easier. Some babies are so tired when it comes
time for a nap that you can put them down awake and have
them happily drift off. Others need to be nurtured in your arms
until they fall asleep, and then you can put them in their crib, as
described in the previous tip. "Somehow the crib didn't seem

like such a bad place to her at night once she was comfortable sleeping in it during the day," says Natalie, who started wean-ing her child from the family bed at six months.

Read All About It: Since our focus is on the fam-ily bed, space precludes us from delving into all the ways to help any baby (not just a family bedder) sleep better. But your local bookstore or library is home to plenty of parenting books that contain this kind of information. (We're not talking about the numerous cry-it-out books out there, just books that give tips on how to comfort babies day and night.) Some will be helpful, others less than informative. We recommend spending some time perusing them until you come up with one that seems like a good fit.

Do This Only if You're Desperate: Many parents are tempted by the lure of numerous popular sleep-training books that advocate letting infants cry it out alone in their cribs so they can learn to sleep for long periods. The techniques are harsh, sometimes calling for babies to cry for as long as it takes in order for them to learn that no one will come help them, and that they may as well fall asleep.

For numerous reasons we don't like these techniques (see pages 93–104 for more about this issue). But we realize that some family bed parents may get desperate enough to resort to them regardless of what we say. For these parents we offer a sleep-training technique that is kinder and gentler. It's not something we want to recommend, since some crying is often involved. In fact, we thought long and hard about whether or not to include it in the book. But we finally opted to, in hopes that desperate parents would choose this more humane method over the many grueling ones out there.

(Note: Since Dr. Jay came up with this method as a more empathetic alternative to the harsher cry-it-out-alone techniques, the following section is a direct "prescription" from him.)

Ten Nights

There are dozens of confusing books and magazine articles implying that there can be some quick and easy way to get your baby to sleep or to not nurse through the night. I have yet to read one that told parents the complete truth: It's not easy, it's rarely quick, and it's usually a little loud and heartbreaking for a few nights . . . or more. I have seen too many families needing help and getting offered choices they didn't like at all.

There should be a third choice to the dichotomy of crying it out or giving in to all-night nursing, and there is. Babies wake up for the optimal interaction with their moms: breast-feeding back to sleep. If we offer them a little less than that for a few nights and then a little less and still less in the ensuing nights, gentle behavior modification will lead them to realize that it might not be worth it to knock on the door of a closed restaurant, so to speak.

Here's what I recommend (and please keep in mind that I like what you're doing now much better than what I'm going to spell out here, but I'd rather see you do this than use a typical cry-it-out technique):

First, do this only if your baby is at least twelve months

old, and is wonderfully healthy. Before anything, consider if this is something you really want to do. As we mentioned earlier in the chapter, don't change your sleeping setup because a friend, relative, or doctor thinks it's the right time. You pick your time.

If you still really need to stop the night waking, read on.

Choose the most valuable seven hours of sleep for yourselves. I personally prefer 11:00 P.M. through 6:00 A.M., but you might have a slightly different idea.

Change the rules during those hours and be comfortable that a "well-built" family bed baby's personality can withstand this rule-changing and the mild inconsistency of getting everything he wants all the time ... ooops, almost all the time. That's the word we want to show this baby. The word "almost." It would be great if we could explain to him that "tired moms and dads aren't as much fun as they could be." If that explanation only made sense to kids somewhere before the third birthday (and it doesn't!), they would simply roll over, say, "See you in the morning," and let us get the sleep we want.

I try to do this in three- and four-night intervals.

I'm assuming that both parents agree—or almost agree—that this is the best thing to do. And the most important assumption of all is that you're willing to go "in a straight line" to the goal of seven straight hours of sleep.

The reason for that last statement is this: If your baby learns that crying, squirming, and fussing (euphemisms, let's just say "crying") will get him fed, you will set yourself back quite a bit. This is a kinder alternative to other cry-it-out sleep-training methods, but it's far from easy.

You should be forewarned that while this technique usually takes ten nights to create significant and long-lasting change, it's not magic and can take longer—another week or more in some cases. What I give you here is the outline for how it typically works in ten nights.

The First Three Nights

First, is it better to do this in the family bed, a crib in the same room, or using a crib in another room? I prefer to continue the family bed even though it might seem harder at first. Some people have better luck setting up a crib in the room and taking the baby in and out. This has always seemed harder to me, but it might be the method you choose. My least favorite choice is a separate bedroom. Even so, this might be the best choice for your family if it feels right.

At any time before 11:00 P.M. (including 10:58) nurse your child to sleep, cuddle and nurse when he wakes up and nurse him back to sleep. But "close the door" at 11:00 P.M. and don't nurse or cuddle or walk him back to sleep. Instead, when your baby awakens at midnight or any other time after 11:00 P.M., hug him, nurse him for a short time, but make sure he does not fall asleep on the breast. Then put him down awake. Rub and pat and cuddle a little until he falls asleep, but don't put him back on the breast (or give him a bottle if that's what you've been doing). He must fall asleep on his own.

Now he will probably tell you that he is angry and intensely dislikes this new routine. I believe him. He will also try to tell you that he's scared. I believe he's angry, but a baby who's had hundreds of nights in a row of cuddling is not scared falling asleep with your hand on his back and your voice in his ear. Angry, yes. Scared, no, not really.

During these first three nights, repeat this pattern only after he has slept. He might sleep for fifteen minutes or he might sleep for four hours, but he has to go to sleep and reawaken to get cuddled and fed again.

These will be hard nights.

You may have decided you're really not ready to do this. That's OK. Stop and start over again in a few months if you like. Or don't. Choosing the right time is crucial.

Again, during these first three nights, between 11:00 P.M. and 6:00 A.M., feed for a short time, cuddle, put him down awake, rub, pat, talk until he falls asleep and repeat this cycle only after he's slept and reawakened. At 6:01 A.M., do whatever you have been doing as a morning routine, ignoring the previous seven hours' patterns. Many babies will roll over, nurse, and cuddle back to sleep and give you an extra hour or so. Some won't.

For me, one of the most reassuring parts of this "sleep plan" is seeing that babies wake up fine, happy, and grudge-free about the change in the rules. You'll see what I mean, even if the first few minutes of the morning are not exactly as they've always been.

The Second Three Nights

Again, the metaphorical door closes at 11:00 P.M. When your baby wakes up, hug and cuddle him for a few minutes, but do not feed him. Put him down awake. Putting him down awake is a crucial part of this whole endeavor because it really does teach him to fall asleep with a little less contact, and then a little less. Not feeding is the big change during these three nights. Older babies can easily go for those seven hours (or more) with no calories. They like to get fed a little through the night, but physiologically and nutritionally this is not a long time to go without food.

If I could wake my wife a few times each night, ask her to squeeze me a little fresh orange juice (my favorite drink) and rub my back while I drank it, I wouldn't choose to voluntarily give up this routine. My wife might have some different ideas and get tired of the pattern quickly. Babies rarely give up their favorite patterns and things—day or night—without balking and crying.

I really don't like listening to babies cry. I actually hate listening to babies crying. Unlike them, though, we adults can truly understand the implications of lack of sleep for a family of three, four, or more people. Sleep patterns sometimes have to be changed and the incredible safety and reassurance the family bed has provided, and continues to provide, supplies the best context and location for these changes.

During these second three nights, some babies will cry and protest for ten minutes at a time and some will go for longer. This is hard, but it will work. I believe that a well-loved baby, after a year or more in the family bed, will be the ultimate beneficiary of his parents getting more sleep. Not coincidentally, the parents benefit, too.

By the end of the sixth night, your baby is going back to sleep without being nursed or fed. He's going back to sleep after a nice hug, a cuddle, and with your hand on his back and your words in his ear.

The Next Four Nights

Nights seven, eight, nine, and ten: Don't pick him up, don't hug him. When he awakens after 11:00 P.M., talk to him, touch him, talk some more, but don't pick the baby up. Rub and pat only. No feeding either, obviously. He will fall back to sleep. Repeat the rubbing and talking when he reawakens. By the end of the ninth night, he will be falling back to sleep, albeit reluctantly for some babies and toddlers, with only a rub and a soothing voice.

After

After these first ten nights, continue to cuddle and feed to sleep if you like and if he wants to, but do nothing when he wakes up except to touch a little and talk to him briefly. This may continue for another three or four nights but occasionally keeps going for another week or more. Then . . . it stops. The baby has learned that he is just as well-loved, gets virtually everything he needs and wants all day, but must give seven hours per night back to his parents and family.

What happens if you travel, the baby gets sick, or some other circumstance demands a return to more nighttime inter-action? Nothing. You do what you need to do (cuddle, nurse, walk, in the middle of the night, as many times as you need to) and then spend a night or two or three getting back to the new pattern the family has established.

By the way, pay the baby. Make sure that he really does get a lot of the benefit of your getting a good night's sleep. Go to the park more often. Do all those things with him you said you'd do if he ever let you sleep longer. Explain it to him as you're doing it. Your baby will understand in an ever-increasing way and will be OK with all this.

A Very Special Place

Congratulations! You gave your child the most tender, nurturing, very best start in life by opening your arms and your bed to him at night when he needed you most. And now he's moved on, just as you knew he'd have to do one day (although you may have doubted he ever would!).

So there you are, on your own for the first time in months, maybe years. It's feeling pretty roomy, eh? Pretty big. Pretty empty.

Getting used to sleeping without your child can be difficult. Ghosts of morning smiles, sweet baby breath, and endless tender and fun moments are powerful—and not inclined to vanish overnight. Even though your child may be in the next room, or just in another bed in your room, the empty nest syndrome can really come home to roost when your little love is no longer snuggling beside you at night.

"That first night he slept in his own bed was weird, weird, weird," says Macall, mother of three family bed children. "I didn't sleep well that night."

Cheryl, whose youngest child left the family bed a few years ago, shared Macall's feeling of loss. "I cried when I took the bed rail down," she recalls. "I knew this was almost the end of an era of my life, a time that would never come again (except grandchildren!)."

But just because your child now sleeps in his own space, don't assume he won't be visiting the family bed again. As we mentioned earlier, the weaning process is often a back-and-forth one, with a child spending some time on his own, some in the family bed.

As your child gets more used to sleeping on his own, so will you.

That doesn't mean you'll forget your fond family bed memories. In fact, the memories of less pleasant events, like waking up to football-like kicks in the kidney all night, tend to fade, leaving more room for the magical ones. Jane, mother of four children from twenty-four to ten years old, says her family's co-sleeping memories continue to be very special. "We all miss sleeping together. We talk about it fondly. My husband and I cuddle with the dachshund and reminisce about the babies," she says.

Many families maintain the "open-bed policy" we described earlier, in which the children know they're welcome back into the family bed whenever they want and for whatever reason. It makes the transition easier for everyone. And it's a way to savor one of the sweetest times in your life a little longer.

Like many parents of family bed "graduates," Mary, a mother of five, says some of her fondest family bed times have actually happened after her children were long gone from the family bed. "We have always had our bed as the central part of our home. . . . It is the place that we all come to that is our together place. Our older children, when still living at home, would still come there to tell us of their lives.

"It is where our daughter told us she had become engaged.

Good Nights

In fact our son-in-law-to-be came in there to tell us, too," says Mary. (Now that's what we call an extended family bed!)

These visits to the old family bed tend to bring out communication in older children that most parents can only dream of. Many remarkably open talks have been shared by parents and returning family bed "graduates" during the magic twilight hours of sleep.

Justine, mother of three family bed "graduates" now in their twenties, says the family bed continues to play an extraordinary role in her relationship with her children: "My girls frequently still sleep in my bed with me when they're home—preceded, of course, by some long, intimate, heart-to-heart conversations that take place so naturally in a dark room late at night with one scented candle lit and snuggled up to Mom."

We hope the family bed will continue to be a very special place for you and your family—whether with return visits or happy memories. Hats off to you for giving your child the most wonderful start to a most wonderful life.

8.

Bedtime Stories
Reassuring Reading from
Real Family Bedders

Z Z Z Z Z Z Z Z Z Z Z Z Z Z Z Z Z Z Z

Since many family bed parents worry about how their children will turn out, you may find it comforting to hear from people who slept in the family bed as babies and children. Most of them are family bed "graduates." Most wouldn't trade the memories and the benefits of their co-sleeping nights for all the cribs in the Western world.

Turn here when you need a little boost, some incentive to keep following your instincts, some experienced hands—big and little--to hold when doubts weigh heavy in the dark of night.

We think you'll come away realizing that good nights truly do beget happy days—and even years and lifetimes.

A NOTE FROM DR. JAY: *I can personally attest to just how great these kids turn out. In my practice, which is rife with family bedders, I have so few teenagers in trouble, so few kids who go through large emotional*

Good Nights

crises. *I sometimes have to reread articles about the percentages of kids with various problems because I don't see them. If there is a problem, parents of these children are so close to them that they can see it early and take care of it or get their child help before things get out of hand. Allowing them to be very dependent when they need to be dependent encourages them to be independent when the time is right. How nice that is.*

 "I enjoyed and remember this time very well. Every night when I went to bed I felt as if nothing could hurt me. In other words, I felt very secure.... I liked sleeping between both parents because I felt invincible."

—BRITTON, 10

 "I felt so safe in the family bed.... Why would a small child want to sleep by itself in the dark, behind bars?"

—SARAH, 17

 "I always knew that my parents were there for me with open arms. They didn't believe that their jobs as parents ended as soon as my head hit the pillow."

—JENNIFER, 28,

MOM OF A FAMILY BED BABY OF HER OWN

"*I feel closer to my parents because I co-slept. I remember the closeness I felt to my parents and the love they shared with my brother and me.*"

—TODD, 22

"*I felt safer 'cause when you are little you don't care that you are sleeping with your parents. It doesn't mean you are a wuss. . . . No little kid would want to sleep alone unless they have to. There might be monsters under the bed or little noises in the house or outside.*"

—ALLEN, 16

"*Even after I left the bed 'full time,' I remember cozy Sunday mornings cuddling with my parents while they read the paper in bed, being read stories, and having long talks with my mom. As I got older, that would often be when I felt closest to her and could confide in her the most.*"

—CATHERINE, 23

"*Babies and young children should definitely sleep with their mommy and daddy. . . . I can't stand when I baby-sit and the parents tell me just to let the baby cry itself to sleep in a crib. It is so sad to hear it. . . . I want to have my children sleep with me 'til they're like three or four. . . . But not until I'm older.*"

—JORDAN, 14

Good Nights

 "I remember that waking-up time was generally a time for laughter. That was always a lot of fun."

—ELIZABETH, 13

 "I always felt extremely comforted [being in the family bed]. . . . There were lots of people and limbs to get tangled up in. I'm very close to my family, and co-sleeping was definitely part of it. . . . A lot of my security probably comes from being able to sleep in the family bed."

—RACHEL, 16

 "I always knew my parents were there day or night to comfort and care for me. That has made me more independent and confident."

—RACHELLE, 22

 "Our family is very close, and I know that co-sleeping had a lot to do with it. We are also very sensitive to others' needs, something we learned from our parents.

"My parents' favorite story is when I was about 6 months old, and I rolled in the wrong direction to nurse—on my dad. He woke up with a start when I actually latched on. He said that was the last night he ever slept without a shirt on."

—GENEVIEVE, 22,

MOTHER OF A FAMILY BED BABY OF HER OWN

"I think a child feels better about going to sleep at night if they know that they don't have to go into a big dark room all alone. Instead they can look forward to going to bed with mom and dad and not having to worry about the 'monster in the closet.'"

—TIM, 13

"I remember my dad telling my brother and me Scooby Doo stories while falling asleep in his arms. This occurred every night except when he worked late. The family bed gave me a feeling of closeness. It's something all families should feel, yet very few do."

—STEVEN, 18

"I am closer to my parents because of the family bed.... I think all humans naturally want to sleep near someone and not alone. I am comfortable by myself now, but it is nice every now and then to sleep in the same room with my parents."

—JAY, 12

"I liked it and I didn't like it. The reason I liked it is it felt safe. When I had nightmares and would wake up in the middle of the night crying, I didn't have to scream to get my mom and dad. It gave me a good idea of what good parenting should be. The reasons I didn't like it were my dad snored, and I got kicked a lot."

—LEILA, 14

Good Nights

 "A great memory is seeing my mom in the middle of the night."

—JUSTIN, 6

 "I loved sleeping in my parents' bed. I felt safe. It was cozy."

—JULIE, 15

 "Sometimes I got up early with my dad and ate breakfast with him and then got back in bed with mom. I liked to get really, really close to mom. She was so warm, and I could get warm."

—MELIA, 14

 "I remember as a small child how nice it was to have my grandmother to cuddle up to whenever I had a bad dream. I also remember scooting my foot over against her leg and keeping it there as I was falling asleep to reassure myself that she was still there. She snored, and I remember finding this sound very reassuring as well, since it also meant that I was not alone."

—ZAN, 40,

MOTHER OF FOUR CHILDREN WHO ALL SHARED HER BED

 "I felt totally safe and happy. My favorite memory is that my mom read us stories every night. I would snuggle up next to her and usually fall asleep during the story. I learned to read this way since she followed the words with her finger."

—KRISTA, 25

"Everyone used to crawl into mom's and dad's king-sized bed in the early morning hours. My youngest siblings usually slept there during the early dawn hours, but even us older kids would usually climb in there once we woke up. I remember being around 14 years old, snuggling and playing with my three younger siblings while mom and dad attempted to squeeze in a few more minutes of sleep and wondering what in the world would my friends think if they knew I was hanging out in my parents' bed. But I felt so warm and secure in there with the entire family that I didn't really care what they thought. Those are some of my happiest memories, and I know they will be among the happiest of my kids' memories because I see the joy in their faces when we all snuggle together in the family bed on lazy weekend mornings."

— LAURA, 26,

MOTHER OF TWO FAMILY BED CHILDREN OF HER OWN

 "Bedtime was a nice time for talking and joking with the whole family. My brother made his first joke at around 6 months, when we were all sitting on the bed. He pointed to mom's breast and said 'appa juice.'"

—BECKY, 26

 "I liked to snuggle down in the covers with my parents. It felt so so so comfortable."

—EMMA, 9

Good Nights

 "A great memory is seeing my mom in the middle of the night."

—JUSTIN, 6

"I loved sleeping in my parents' bed. I felt safe. It was cozy."

—JULIE, 15

 "Sometimes I got up early with my dad and ate breakfast with him and then got back in bed with mom. I liked to get really, really close to mom. She was so warm, and I could get warm."

—MELIA, 14

"I remember as a small child how nice it was to have my grandmother to cuddle up to whenever I had a bad dream. I also remember scooting my foot over against her leg and keeping it there as I was falling asleep to reassure myself that she was still there. She snored, and I remember finding this sound very reassuring as well, since it also meant that I was not alone."

—ZAN, 40,
MOTHER OF FOUR CHILDREN WHO ALL SHARED HER BED

"I felt totally safe and happy. My favorite memory is that my mom read us stories every night. I would snuggle up next to her and usually fall asleep during the story. I learned to read this way since she followed the words with her finger."

—KRISTA, 25

"My parents' bed was a welcome place for any of us. I cherish the memories of having my brother near me at night. When my sisters who are 11 and 14 years younger than I were toddlers, they would often sleep with me. I loved that."

—KATERI, 31,

MOTHER OF TWO FAMILY BED CHILDREN

 "I like it when I've been bad in the mornings and at night people forgive me because I get hugs and kisses in bed. I like it because my sister is cute in the morning and she runs over the bed and stands on my brother when he is asleep. If your bed is real big and your parents sleep with you I feel they love me more."

—LIZA, 5

 "It made me feel great. It made me feel a lot safer."

—DÁVID, 6

 "The family bed was a very important part of my growing up. Even after my siblings and I outgrew the family bed, we always gathered there in the evenings to watch TV or to talk, and during the day if we wanted to just lay [sic] down. When we were sick we always wanted to be in our parents' bed. I think there was some medicinal value in being in their bed. Even now, all but one of us is grown and moved out of our mother's house, when we go home for a visit, many times we will gather on mom's bed and talk, and cuddle with each other. I think it's a very important part of our lives. It helps to

keep those close ties to each other, and it's very calming to know that mom's bed is always available when I want to talk about something, or just need a hug."

—RACHEL, 22

"I strongly believe that I am the person I am today because of where I slept. I remember those nights more vividly than I remember a few nights ago. It was the safest I think I ever felt. . . . If and when the time comes that I have children, there would be no way I would ever put that child in a crib. I feel that children need to feel safe and protected. No, everyone needs to feel safe and protected:

"When I was 19, my mother was in a horrible car accident and was wheelchair bound for two months. My bedroom was on the other side of the house, so if she needed anything while I was asleep, there was nothing she could do. Every night of those two months I slept in her bed, next to her. Through everything I was there until the cast came off. Why? She mothered me every day of my life, up until that point. I thought she needed a mother right then. If she woke up in the middle of the night crying in pain, I didn't want some 'Mommy-monitor' to let me know. I wanted to be able to turn over and hold her, or get up and go to the store to get her medication."

—SARAH, 21

Afterword

As a family physician who provides both maternity care and well child care, I encounter co-sleeping families every week. Many of them are unaware of the basic safety recommendations for co-sleeping. Many others are afraid to tell their physician about their true sleeping practice for fear of being thought of as a bad parent, or worse, as a child abuser.

Physicians need to be educated on the facts about co-sleeping. This needs to start in medical school. With increased education, we can propose and carry out studies that have the potential to enhance our patients' lives. To show the benefits of co-sleeping and educate parents as to possible dangers, we must start with basic education and a renewed research effort that is free of the biases that have often plagued this sensitive area of investigation. We also need to explore and understand better the link between co-sleeping and breast-feeding in order to encourage this most important method of infant feeding.

This is an area where clinical medicine needs to take the

lead. We must work with patients to come up with solutions that are consistent with their goals and values, as long as the solutions are not proven to be harmful. To ignore a practice that most parents try at some point is to not do them justice.

As a family physician I enjoy working with the whole family. There is nothing more rewarding than watching a family grow up together in a joyful harmonious way. Co-sleeping can be a very important part of that.

—Steve Cohen, M.D.
    Clinical Assistant Professor of Family Medicine
      and Clinical Epidemiology
    University of Pittsburgh School of Medicine
    Director of Predoctoral Education
    UPMC Shadyside Family Practice Residency Program

Appendices

Appendix A: The CPSC
Report—Explaining the Errors

Rather than present you with our views of the problems with the 1999 U.S. Consumer Product Safety Commission report, which some might interpret as biased because of our stand on the family bed, we'll let a couple of objective parties do the analysis.

If you have access to the internet, we highly recommend an article from the electronic edition of the *Western Journal of Medicine* from May 2001: "Evidence Supports Respecting Informed Parental Preference," by Mary Ann O'Hara, senior research fellow at the Department of Family Medicine, University of Washington, Seattle. You can find it at www.ewjm.com/cgi/content/full/174/5/301.

The following excerpt is from a lead article of the

respected medical journal, *Contemporary Pediatrics* (Copyright © 2000, *Contemporary Pediatrics,* a Medical Economics/Thomson Healthcare publication, reproduced with permission):

"The authors of the report, who are employees of the CPSC, acknowledge flaws in their research, such as the incomplete and anecdotal nature of their databases, which depend on information from death certificates that mention a specific consumer product and consumer complaints, as well as media articles and medical emergency services reports. The way the data were collected did not permit the authors to determine how many children co-slept, and hence were at risk of dying while doing so, or the total number of children who died while cosleeping.

"These incomplete databases should lead to underreporting of infant deaths associated with co-sleeping. Because of the way the authors analyze the data, however, they may have overreported such deaths. According to the report, 515 children younger than 2 years who were placed to sleep on adult beds died during an 8-year period (1990–1997). Of these, 121 deaths, or 15 a year, were attributed to overlying by a parent or other family member. The remaining 394 deaths, the authors determined, resulted from suffocation or strangulation when the child's head was caught in a structure of the bed." (*Good Nights* authors' comment: Fully one-fifth of those deaths occurred in water beds, which have long been known as very dangerous places to place a baby to sleep.)

"The most significant flaw in the CPSC's research is how it ascertained the cause of death. Of the infants who reportedly died because of parental suffocation, the authors say they excluded deaths that probably were caused by SIDS but included those caused by overlying, indicated in the databases by descriptions such as 'mother fell asleep while nursing,' 'sleeping mother overlay child's body,' and infant 'accidentally rolled over by mother.'

"We have no way of knowing if these infants really died of SIDS instead of by overlying, as the CPSC claims. In addition, investigators did not collect any information about parental drug, alcohol, or cigarette use. Even more important, the report does not include any information about the number of infants who die in their cribs because of an unsafe sleeping environ-ment. The lay press is appropriately criticizing the government for using flawed research to advocate so strongly that infants should not sleep in an adult bed and for not acknowledging data that demonstrate the possible benefits of co-sleeping."[1]

Appendix B: Helpful Resources

The following organizations and web sites can help you get great co-sleeping information and put you in touch with other parents who use the family bed. Since Web sites come and go, we're listing only a few. But if you log onto our web site, described below, we'll supply plenty of links to related sites.

- First, we'd like to welcome you to visit us at our web site, www.familybed.com. You'll find helpful advice, answers to your questions, and links to other Web sites. At fam-ilybed.com, we do everything but tuck you in to help you get comfortable with the family bed.

Appendices

- James J. McKenna, Ph.D., the father of scientific research on the family bed, maintains a wonderful web site for his Mother-Baby Behavioral Sleep Laboratory at the University of Notre Dame: www.nd.edu/~alfac/mckenna. Among the many items of interest: His answers to frequently asked questions, information on the latest research, co-sleeping news, and McKenna's philosophical reflections. The photos alone are worth a look.

- Countless parenting web sites provide excellent information on all kinds of parenting issues. The two we'll mention here are www.momsonline.com, since Dr. Jay is one of the "pediatric pro's" there, and www.drjaygordon.com, Dr. Jay's very own site. Visit our familybed.com web site, mentioned on page 195, for links to other helpful parenting sites.

- Attachment Parenting International (API) is a very good resource center for information on "attachment" parenting (we prefer to call it natural parenting). Co-sleeping is one of the many natural parenting techniques they espouse. There are several API support groups in the United States, and API is always interested in helping parents form more groups.

Attachment Parenting International
1508 Clairmont Place
Nashville, Tennessee 37215
U.S.A.
615/298-4334
www.attachmentparenting.org
or e-mail for information: info@attachmentparenting.org

• La Leche League International offers three thousand mother-to-mother breast-feeding support group meetings around the world every month. Attend a meeting for breast-feeding support and information, and you'll likely be in the company of other family bedders (although there's no guarantee; not all groups end up having co-sleepers). With so many meeting locations, there's bound to be one near you. The web site and the toll-free line make it easy to hook up with your local group.

La Leche League International
1400 Meacham Road
Schaumburg, Illinois 60173-4048
U.S.A.
847/519-7730
800/LA-LECHE (This line is staffed by volunteer La Leche League leaders from 9:00 A.M. to 5:00 P.M. Central Time, Monday through Friday. You can also leave a message to find out the contact information for your local La Leche group.).
www.lalecheleague.org

Appendix C: About Our Questionnaires/Interviews

It started simply enough. We wanted to talk to parents who sleep or slept next to their babies. Our aim was to find out everything possible, from how the babies ended up in the parents' beds, to how the babies left the beds (if indeed they had yet), and everything else in between.

Our interviews consisted of approximately seventy questions—very few of them with simple "yes" or "no" answers. As
time went on, word of the interviews for our book spread
among family bed parents, thanks to postings with various parents' organizations around the United States and abroad. We
were deluged with requests for interviews. Since each interview took at least ninety minutes, we would probably still be
working on the interviews if we had kept going on that track!
So to save time, we turned our interview questions into a questionnaire and sent it out to parents via e-mail and regular mail.

In the end we interviewed and received questionnaires
back from approximately 250 parents. It is the largest and most
extensive compilation of this kind of data so far.

We also developed a much shorter questionnaire for
children of the family bed. We got back approximately fifty
of these completed questionnaires. Almost all of the children
had "graduated" from the bed. And several of these "children"
were now adults. The information we obtained from these
questionnaires was also groundbreaking, revealing an extremely
positive side of co-sleeping.

Our research also called for an exploration of sleep habits
around the world. As part of this, we developed a questionnaire for parents from countries other than the United States
and Canada. This resulted in about twenty-five responses.

You'll read about the experiences of dozens of these family
bedders throughout the book. Every person you read about in
this book is real. To protect their privacy, we use first names
only, and rarely any other identifying information, such as
where they live or occupation. In the chapter on sex, we don't
use names at all. Nor do we use names when parents bemoan
their critics in the chapter on coping with criticism. (We had

indicated in the questionnaire and when we spoke with parents that this would be the case. This may help account for the very candid responses we received.)

In some cases we tabulated the answers to certain questions and used a percentage figure indicating our findings—or a more general indicator of percentage ("vast majority," for example) when it was impossible to come up with an exact figure because of the complexity of some of the answers. But for the most part, we mined these questionnaires and interviews for experiences, for advice, and for the words of these family bedders. The territory was rich, as you will see throughout the book.

The parents who contacted us come from all walks of life. Many are stay-at-home moms, but there are also physicians, professors, students, lawyers, teachers, cooks, stay-at-home dads, and dozens of other professions. Most are married, but we heard from a few single parents and same-sex couples. Some of our respondents have only one child, many have two or three, and a surprising number have four or more. (One even has had fifty, counting foster children!) Most who responded to our questionnaire appear to be middle to upper-middle class. This may be partly because so many parents learned of our research via their home computers.

While our questionnaires and interviews were not as scientific as they would have been if we had known from the outset that we were looking for numbers as well as quotes, they provided us with more magnificent information than we could have dreamed of for our purposes. We hope our findings spur other researchers to delve into this line of investigation, perhaps with a more quantitative bent. The family bedders are out there. They want to talk. And it's time for them to be heard.

Notes

Chapter 1: Baby Knows Best

1. McKenna et al., 1993.
2. McKenna, 1993.
3. Trevathan, 1987.
4. Trevathan, 1999.
5. Field, 1998.
6. Lewis et al., 2000.
7. McKenna, 1986.
8. Hofer, 1981.
9. Heller, 1997, p. 35.
10. Anderson, 1991.
11. Gray et al., 2000.
12. Schanberg and Field, 1987.
13. Lewis et al., 2000, pp. 69–70.
14. Mosko, Richard, McKenna, Drummond, 1996.
15. McKenna et al., 1990.
16. Mosko et al., 1993.
17. Mosko et al., 1997.
18. McKenna, 1996. *Annual Review of Anthropology.*
19. Sears and Sears, 1993, p. 595.

Notes

20. Konner and Super, 1987.
21. Fujita, et al., 1998.
22. Harlow et al., 1973.
23. Insel, 1992.
24. Anders and Taylor, 1994.
25. Hooker et al., 2000.
26. McKenna et al., 1997.
27. Mosko, Richard, McKenna, 1996.
28. Keefe, 1988.
29. McKenna, 1996. *World Health*.
30. Litt, 1981.
31. Wolf and Lozoff, 1989.
32. Gaddini and Gaddini, 1971.
33. Hong and Townes, 1976.
34. Ozturk and Ozturk, 1977.
35. Hayes et al., 1996.
36. Ferber, 1985, pp. 40–41.
37. Wolf and Lozoff, 1989.
38. Anders and Taylor, 1994.
39. Lozoff et al., 1985.
40. Anders, 1994.
41. Kaplan and Poznanski, 1974.
42. McKenna, 1996. *World Health*.
43. Heron, 1994.
44. Mosenkis, 1998.
45. Forbes and Weiss, 1992.
46. Lewis and Janda, 1988.
47. Based on our questionnaire and interviews with family bed graduates (see appendix C for more on our research).
48. Ainsworth, 1982.
49. Ainsworth, 1985.
50. Wolf and Lozoff, 1989.
51. Lewis et al., 2000, pp. 196–97.
52. Ferber, 1985, pp. 38–39.
53. Seabrook, 1999.
54. Heron, 1994.
55. Forbes and Weiss, 1992.

56. Based on our questionnaire and interviews with family bed graduates (see appendix C for more on our research).
57. Konner, 1981.
58. Wolf et al., 1996.
59. Thevenin, 1987, p. 58.
60. Gathorne-Hardy, 1973.
61. Thevenin, 1987, p. 58.
62. McKenna, 2000. *Sleep and Breathing in Children.*
63. Jackson, 1999, pp. 56–58.
64. Jackson, 1999, pp. 60–62.
65. Thevenin, 1987, p. 59.

Chapter 2: Tales from the Crib

1. Ross Mothers' Survey, 1999.
2. Hooker, et al., 2000.

Chapter 3: Practicing Safe Sleep

1. Nakamura et al., 1999.
2. Lane, 1999.
3. Nakamura et al., 1999.
4. Consumer Product Safety Commission, 1999.
5. McKenna, 2000. *Contemporary Pediatrics.*
6. Drago and Dannenberg, 1999.
7. Consumer Product Safety Commission, 2001.
8. Nakamura et al., 1999.
9. American SIDS Institute.
10. Blair et al., 1999.
11. American SIDS Institute.
12. McLaughlin, 1988, p. 120.
13. McLaughlin, 1988, pp. 156–157.
14. Fildes, 1986, p. 196.
15. Hrdy, 1999, p. 291.

Notes

Chapter 4: The Sandman Cometh

1. Morelli, et al., 1992.
2. Singer, 1999.
3. Jones et al., 1999.
4. Singer, 1999.
5. Elias et al., 1986.
6. Elias et al., 1986.
7. Wolfson et al., 1992.
8. Hall, 1998.
9. Sears, 1985, p. 81.
10. Mindell, 1997, p. 112.
11. Ferber, 1985, p. 74.
12. Pearce, 1999, p. 70.
13. Weissbluth, 1987, p. 157.
14. Ferber, 1985, p. 194.
15. Mindell, 1997, p. 230.
16. Weissbluth, 1987, p. 202.
17. Coe et al., 1985.
18. Reite and Capitanio, 1985.
19. Seabrook, 1999.
20. Zero to Three, 2000.
21. Zero to Three, 2000.
22. Ainsworth, 1977.
23. Coe et al., 1985.

Chapter 5: Love in the Laundry Room

1. Mindell, 1997, p. 76.
2. Westheimer and Grunebaum, 1999, p. 226.
3. *Home & Garden Television*, 1998.
4. Insel, 1992.
5. Insel, 1992.
6. Thevenin, 1987, p. 115.

Notes

Chapter 6: Critical Support

1. Cited in Jackson, 1999, p. 49.
2. *60 Minutes*, 1999.
3. Jewel, 1999.
4. Schneider and Blonska, 1999.
5. *Home & Garden Television*, 1998.
6. Hotchner, 1979, p. 26.
7. Goldman, 1981, p. 68.
8. Wolf et al., 1996.
9. Barry and Paxson, 1971.
10. Wolf et al., 1996.
11. Shweder et al., 1995.
12. Morelli et al., 1992.
13. Morelli et al., 1992.
14. Shweder et al., 1995.
15. McKenna, 2000.
16. Caudill and Plath, 1996.
17. New, 1988.
18. Wolf et al., 1996.

Chapter 7: A Farewell to Arms—and Legs ... and Feet ...

1. Sinrod, 1993, p. 13.

Appendix A: The CPSC Report—Explaining the Errors

1. Anderson, 2000.

Bibliography

Ainsworth, Mary (1985). "Patterns of infant-mother attachment: Antecedents and effects on development," and "Attachments across the life-span." *Bulletin of the New York Academy of Medicine* 61:771–91 and 791–812.

Ainsworth, Mary (1982). "Attachment: Retrospect and prospect," in *The Place of Attachment in Human Behavior*, C.M. Parkes and J. Stevenson-Hinde, eds. New York: Basic Books, 3–30.

Ainsworth, Mary, D. Salter (1977). "Maternal influences on infant-mother attachment," in *Developments in Psychiatric Research*, J.M. Tanner, ed. New York: Hodder and Stoughton, 1–20.

American SIDS Institute. One of several SIDS and pediatric organizations disseminating information about the dangerous correlation between smoking and SIDS. Available at www.sids.org.

Anders, Thomas F. (1994). Cited in "Infant sleep, nighttime relationships, and attachment." *Psychiatry* 57, no. 1:11–21.

Anders, Thomas F., and Teresa R. Taylor (1994). "Babies and their sleep environment." *Children's Environments* 11, no. 2:123–34.

Anderson, Gene C. (1991). "Current knowledge about skin-to-skin (kangaroo) care for preterm infants." *Journal of Perinatology* 11:216–26.

Anderson, Jane E. (2000). "Co-sleeping: Can we ever put the issue to rest?" *Contemporary Pediatrics* 17, no. 6:98–121.

Bibliography

Barry, Herbert, and Leonora M. Paxson (1971). "Infancy and early child-hood: Cross-cultural codes 2." *Ethnology* 10:466–508.

Blair, Peter S., Peter J. Fleming, Iain J. Smith, Martin Ward Platt, Jeanine Young, Pam Nadin, P. J. Berry, and Jean Golding (1999). "Babies sleeping with parents: Case-control study of factors influencing the risk of the sud-den infant death syndrome." *British Medical Journal* 319:1457–62.

Caudill, William, and David W. Plath (1966). "Who sleeps by whom?: Parent-child involvement in urban Japanese families." *Psychiatry* 29:344–66.

Coe, Christopher L., Sandra G. Wiener, Leon T. Rosenberg, and Seymour Levine (1985). "Endocrine and immune responses to separation and mater-nal loss in nonhuman primates," in *The Psychobiology of Attachment and Sep-aration*, M. Reite and T. Field, eds. New York: Academic Press, 163–99.

Consumer Product Safety Commission (2001). News release: "CPSC, Sim-mons announce recall to repair cribs," (February 21). Available at www.cpsc.gov/cpscpub/prerel/prhtml01/01087.html

Consumer Product Safety Commission (1999). News release: "CPSC warns against placing babies in adult beds," (September 29). Available at www.cpsc.gov/cpscpub/prerel/prhtml99/99175.html

Drago, Dorothy A., and Andrew L. Dannenberg (1999). "Infant mechanical suffocation deaths in the United States, 1980–1997." *Pediatrics* 103, no. 5: E-59. (Electronic article.)

Elias, Marjorie F., Nancy A. Nicolson, Carolyn Bora, and Johanna Johnston (1986). Cited in "Sleep/wake patterns of breast-fed infants in the first two years of life." *Pediatrics* 77, no. 3:322–29.

Ferber, Richard (1985). *Solve Your Child's Sleep Problems*. New York: Simon & Schuster.

Field, Tiffany M. (1998). Cited in "Massage therapy effects." *American Psy-chologist* 35, no. 12:1270–81. This paper summarizes the many studies on massage's effects on infants.

Fildes, Valerie (1986). Cited in *Breasts, Bottles and Babies*. Edinburgh: Edin-burgh University Press.

Forbes, John Francis, and David Shannon Weiss (1992). "The cosleeping habits of military children." *Military Medicine* 157, no. 4:196–200.

Fujita, T., T. Sawaguchi, and A. Sawaguchi (1998). "An epidemiological sur-vey of sudden infant death syndrome in Tokyo." *Nippon Koshu Eisei Zasshi* 45, no. 2: 142–50.

Gaddini, Renata, and Eugenio Gaddini (1970). "Transitional objects and the process of individuation: A study in three different social groups." *Journal of the American Academy of Child Psychiatry* 9:347–65.

Gathorne-Hardy, Jonathan (1973). *The Unnatural History of the Nanny*. New York: Dial Press. References throughout book to the powerful position of the British nanny.

Goldman, Albert (1981). *Elvis*. New York: McGraw-Hill.

Gray, Larry, Lisa Watt, and Elliott M. Blass (2000). "Skin-to-skin contact is analgesic in healthy newborns." *Pediatrics* 105, no. 1:E–14. (Electronic article.)

Hall, Joseph (1998). "Baby cribs breed social ills, psychiatrist says." *Toronto Star* (February 27): F–5.

Harlow, Harry F., Philip E. Plubell, and Craig M. Baysinger (1973). "Induction of psychological death in rhesus monkeys." *Journal of Autism and Childhood Schizophrenia* 3: 299–307.

Hayes, Marie J., Shawn M. Roberts, and Rebecca Stowe (1996). "Early childhood co-sleeping: Parent-child and parent-infant nighttime interactions." *Infant Mental Health Journal* 17, no. 4:348–57.

Heller, Sharon (1997). *The Vital Touch*. New York: Henry Holt. This book contains dozens of examples of how touch affects the well-being of infants.

Heron, P. (1994). "Nonreactive co-sleeping and child behavior: Getting a good night's sleep all night and every night." Masters thesis, University of Bristol, Bristol, United Kingdom. Cited in McKenna, James J. (2000). "Cultural influences on infant and childhood sleep biology and the science that studies it," in *Sleep and Breathing in Children: A Developmental Approach*, G. M. Loughlin, J. L. Carroll, and C. L. Marcus, eds. New York: Marcel Dekker, 99–130.

Hofer, Myron A. (1981). "Parental contributions to the development of their offspring," in *Parental Care in Mammals*, D. J. Gubernick, P. H. Klopfer, eds. New York: Plenum Press, 77–115.

Home & Garden Television special (1998). "At Home with Kenny Loggins."

Hong, K. Michael, and Brenda D. Townes (1976). "Infants' attachment to inanimate objects: A cross-cultural study." *Journal of the American Academy of Child Psychiatry* 15:49–61.

Hooker, Elaine, Helen L. Ball, and Peter J. Kelly (2000). "Sleeping like a baby: Attitudes and experiences of bedsharing in northeast England." *Medical Anthropology* 19, no. 3: 203–22.

Bibliography

Hotchner, A. E. (1979). *Sophia: Living and Loving*. New York: William Morrow.

Hrdy, Sarah Blaffer (1999). Cited in *Mother Nature: Maternal Instincts and How They Shape the Human Species*. New York: Ballantine Books.

Insel, Thomas R. (1992). Cited in "Oxytocin—a neuropeptide for affiliation: evidence from behavioral, receptor, autoradiographic, and comparative studies." *Psychoneuroendocrinology* 17, no. 1:3–35.

Jackson, Deborah (1999). *Three in a Bed*. London: Bloomsbury Press.

Jewel, Dan (1999). "Gift of love: Roberto Benigni's own father inspired *Life is Beautiful*." *People Weekly* 51, no. 9:101–2.

Jones, Christopher R., Scott S. Campbell, Stephanie E. Zone, Fred Cooper, Alison DeSano, Patricia Murphy, Bryan Jones, Laura Czajkowski, and Louis J. Ptacek (1999). "Familial advanced sleep-phase syndrome: A short-period circadian rhythm variant in humans." *Nature Medicine* 5, no. 9:1062–65.

Kaplan, Stuart L., and Elva Poznanski (1974). "Child psychiatric patients who share a bed with a parent." *Journal of the American Academy of Child Psychiatry* 13, no. 2:344–56.

Keefe, Maureen (1988). "The impact of rooming-in on maternal sleep at night." *Journal of Obstetric, Gynecologic, and Neonatal Nursing* 17:122–26.

Konner, Melvin J., and Charles M. Super (1987). "Sudden infant death syndrome: An anthropological hypothesis," in *The Role of Culture in Developmental Disorder*. S. Harkness and C. Super, eds. New York: Academic Press, 95–108.

Konner, Melvin J. (1981). "Evolution of human behavior development," in *Handbook of Cross-Cultural Human Development*. R. H. Munroe, R. L. Munroe, and B. B. Whiting, eds. New York: Garland Press, 3–50.

Lane, Laura (1999). "Commission recommends against children sleeping in adult beds," on WebMD Web site (September 29). Available at www.cnn.com/health/9909/29/adult.bed.journal.wmd/index.html

Lewis, Robin J., and Louis H. Janda (1988). "The relationship between adult sexual adjustment and childhood experiences regarding exposure to nudity, sleeping in the parental bed, and parental attitudes toward sexuality." *Archives of Sexual Behavior* 17, no. 4:349–62.

Lewis, Thomas, Fari Amini, and Richard Lannon (2000). *A General Theory of Love*. New York: Random House. This book is replete with examples of the importance of physiological touch.

Litt, Carole J. (1981). "Children's attachment to transitional objects: A study of two pediatric populations." *American Journal of Orthopsychiatry* 51, no. 1:131–39.

Lozoff, Betsy, Abraham W. Wolf, and Nancy S. Davis (1985). "Sleep problems seen in pediatric practice." *Pediatrics* 75, no. 3:477–83.

McKenna, James J. (2000). Cited in "Cultural influences on infant and childhood sleep biology and the science that studies it," in *Sleep and Breathing in Children: A Developmental Approach*, G. M. Loughlin, J. L. Carroll, and C. L. Marcus, eds. New York: Marcel Dekker, 99–130.

McKenna, James J. (2000). "In defense of Maya's mother," a sidebar in article by Jane E. Anderson, "Co-sleeping: Can we ever put the issue to rest?" *Contemporary Pediatrics* 17, no. 6:98–121.

McKenna, James, Sarah Mosko, and Christopher Richard (1997). "Bedsharing promotes breastfeeding." *Pediatrics* 100:214–219.

McKenna, James (1996). "Sudden infant death syndrome in cross-cultural perspective: Is infant-parent cosleeping proactive?" *Annual Review of Anthropology* 25:201–16.

McKenna, James J. (1996). "Babies need their mothers beside them." *World Health*, no. 2.

McKenna, James J., Evelyn B. Thoman, Thomas F. Anders, Abraham Sadeh, Vicki L. Schechtman, and Steven F. Glotzbach (1993). "Infant-parent co-sleeping in an evolutionary perspective: Implications for understanding infant sleep development and the Sudden Infant Death Syndrome." *Sleep* 16, no. 3:263–82.

McKenna, James J. (1993). "Co-sleeping," entry in *The Encyclopedia of Sleep and Dreaming*, by Mary Carskadon. New York: MacMillan, 143–48.

McKenna, James J., Sarah Mosko, Claibourne Dungy, and Jan McAnich (1990). "Sleep and arousal patterns of co-sleeping human mother/infant pairs: A preliminary physiological study with implications for the study of sudden infant death syndrome (SIDS)." *American Journal of Physical Anthropology* 83: 331–47.

McKenna, James J. (1986). "An anthropological perspective on the sudden infant death syndrome (SIDS): The role of parental breathing cues and speech breathing adaptations." *Medical Anthropology* 10, no. 1:9–53.

McLaughlin, Mary Martin (1988). "Survivors and surrogates: Children and parents from the ninth to thirteenth centuries," in *The History of Childhood: The Untold Story of Child Abuse*, L. deMause, ed. New York: Peter Bedrick Books, 101–82.

Bibliography

Mindell, Jodi A. (1997). *Sleeping Through the Night*. New York: HarperCollins.

Morelli, Gilda A., David Oppenheim, Barbara Rogoff, and Denise Goldsmith (1992). "Cultural variation in infants' sleeping arrangements: Questions of independence." *Developmental Psychology* 28:604–13.

Mosenkis, J. (1998). "The effects of childhood cosleeping on later life development." Masters thesis, University of Chicago. Cited in McKenna, James J. (2000). "Cultural influences on infant and childhood sleep biology and the science that studies it," in *Sleep and Breathing in Children: A Developmental Approach*, G. M. Loughlin, J. L. Carroll, and C. L. Marcus, eds. New York: Marcel Dekker, 99–130.

Mosko, Sarah, Christopher Richard, James McKenna, Sean Drummond, and David Mukai (1997). "Maternal proximity and infant CO_2 environment during bedsharing and possible implications for SIDS research." *American Journal of Physical Anthropology* 103:315–28.

Mosko, Sarah, Christopher Richard, and James McKenna (1996). "Maternal sleep and arousals during bedsharing with infants." *Sleep* 20:142–50.

Mosko, Sarah, Christopher Richard, James McKenna, and Sean Drummond (1996). "Infant sleep architecture during bedsharing and possible implications for SIDS." *Sleep* 19:677–84.

Mosko, Sarah, James McKenna, Michael Dickel, and Lynn Hunt (1993). "Parent-infant co-sleeping: The appropriate context for the study of infant sleep and implications for sudden infant death syndrome (SIDS) research." *Journal of Behavioral Medicine* 16, no. 6:589–610.

Nakamura, Suad, Marilyn Wind, and Mary Ann Danello (1999). "Review of hazards associated with children placed in adult beds." *Archives of Pediatrics & Adolescent Medicine* 153, no. 10:1019–23.

New, Rebecca S. (1988). "Parental goals and Italian infant care," in *Parental Behaviors in Diverse Societies*, R. A. LeVine, P. M. Miller, M. M. West, eds. San Francisco: Jossey-Bass, 51–63.

Ozturk, Mualla, and Orhan M. Ozturk (1977). "Thumbsucking and falling asleep." *British Journal of Medical Psychology* 50:95–103.

Pearce, John (1999). *Baby & Toddler Sleep Program*. Tucson: Fisher Books.

Reite, Martin, and John P. Capitanio (1985). "On the nature of social separation and social attachment," in *The Psychobiology of Attachment and Separation*, M. Reite and T. Field, eds. New York: Academic Press, 223–55.

Ross Mothers' Survey, "Breastfeeding trends through 1998," a report on breastfeeding in the United States, based on an ongoing mail survey (since

Bibliography

1955) by the Ross Products Division of Abbott Laboratories.

Schanberg, Saul, and Tiffany Field (1987). "Sensory deprivation stress and supplemental stimulation in the rat pup and preterm human neonate." *Child Development* 58:1431–47.

Schneider, Karen S., and Joanna Blonska (1999). "Love in vain." *People Weekly* 51, no. 4:70–78.

Seabrook, John (1999). "Sleeping with the baby." *The New Yorker* (November 8):56–65.

Sears, William, and Martha Sears (1993). *The Baby Book*. New York: Little, Brown.

Sears, William (1985). *Nighttime Parenting*. New York: Plume.

Shweder, Richard A., Lene Arnett Jensen, and William M. Goldstein (1995). "Who sleeps by whom revisited: A method for extracting the moral goods implicit in practice," in *Cultural Practices as Contexts for Development*, J.J. Goodnow, P.J. Miller, F. Kessel, eds. San Francisco: Jossey-Bass, 21–40.

Singer, Clifford M., and Alfred J. Lewy (1999). "Does our DNA determine when we sleep?" *Nature Medicine* 5, no. 9: 983.

Sinrod, Barry (1993). *Do You Do It When Your Pet's in the Room?* New York: Ballantine.

60 Minutes (1999). An interview with Roberto Benigni (August 15).

Thevenin, Tine (1987). *The Family Bed*. New Jersey: Avery Publishing Group.

Trevathan, Wenda R. (1999). "Evolutionary obstetrics," in *Evolutionary Medicine*, W.R. Trevathan, E.O. Smith, J.J. McKenna, eds. New York: Oxford University Press, 183–207.

Trevathan, Wenda R. (1987). *Human Birth: An Evolutionary Perspective*. New York: Aldine de Gruyter.

Weissbluth, Marc (1987). *Healthy Sleep Habits, Happy Child*. New York: Fawcett-Columbine.

Westheimer, Ruth, and Amos Grunebaum (1999). *Dr. Ruth's Pregnancy Guide for Couples*. New York: Routledge.

Wolf, Abraham W., Betsy Lozoff, Sara Latz, and Roberto Paludetto (1996). "Parental theories in the management of young children's sleep in Japan, Italy, and the United States," in *Parents' Cultural Beliefs Systems*, S. Harkness, C.M. Super, eds. New York: The Guilford Press, 364–84.

Wolf, Abraham W., and Betsy Lozoff (1989). "Object attachment, thumbsucking, and the passage to sleep." *Journal of the American Academy of Child and Adolescent Psychiatry* 28:287–92.

Bibliography

Wolfson, Amy, Patricia Lacks, and Andrew Futterman (1992). "Effects of parent training on infant sleeping patterns, parents' stress, and perceived parental competence." *Journal of Consulting and Clinical Psychology* 60, no. 1:41–48.

Zero to Three (2000). New release: "Survey reveals child development knowledge gap among adults," (October 4). Available at www.zeroto three.org/pr-survey.html

Index

Index

Index

Index

Index